Traditional
HOME PLANS

862 to 5,254 square feet.

© Copyright 1993 by the L.F. Garlinghouse Co., Inc. of Middletown, Connecticut. All rights reserved. None of the contents of this publication may be reproduced in any form or by any means without the prior written permission of the publisher. All home plans and designs contained in this publication, and their construction drawings, are included under this copyright. Printed in the USA.

Library of Congress No.: 92-075092

ISBN: 0-938708-44-9

TABLE OF CONTENTS	
Cover Plan No. 10663	16-17
Popular Full Color Home Designs	1 – 32
Home Plans for Every Lifestyle	33 – 187
Blueprint Order Pages	188 – 192

Bay Windows and Skylights Brighten Tudor

No. 10673

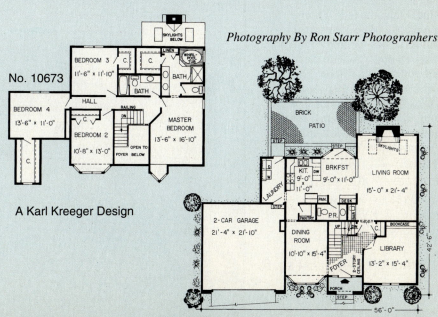

Photography By Ron Starr Photographers

A Karl Kreeger Design

Step from the arched fieldstone porch into the two-story foyer, and you can see that this traditional four bedroom home possesses a wealth of modern elements. Behind double doors lie the library and fireplaced living room, bathed in sunlight from two skylights in the sloping roof. Step out to the brick patio from the laundry room or bay-windowed breakfast room. For ultimate relaxation, the master bedroom suite contains a whirlpool tub. One bedroom boasts bay windows; another features a huge walk-in closet over the two-car garage.

First floor — 1,265 sq. ft.
Second floor — 1,210 sq. ft.
Basement — 1,247 sq. ft.
Garage — 506 sq. ft.

Total living area — 2,475 sq. ft.

No. 10334

Stately Home With An Exceptional Floor Plan

Here's a fabulous home for you and your family. A study, walk-in closet, lavish bath with whirlpool, shower, skylight, and the master suite are exceptional features of this home. The open-railed balcony accents the eye-catching 25 ft. oak-floored Great room with bow window. Also featured are two bedrooms, a slate-floored dining room, and a kitchen with pantry and snack island. On the basement level, the family room joins the patio via sliding glass doors, and a fourth bedroom and extra bath are included.

Main level — 1,742 sq. ft.
Upper level — 809 sq. ft.
Lower level — 443 sq. ft.
Basement — 1,270 sq. ft.
Garage — 558 sq. ft.

Total living area — 2,994 sq. ft.

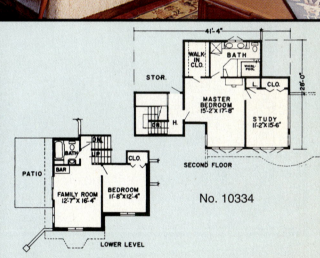

No. 10334

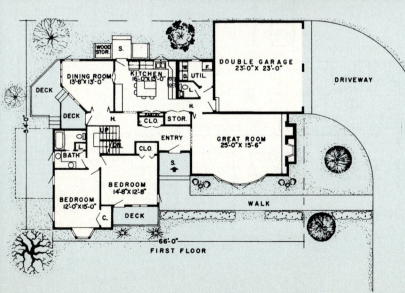

Thinking About Space And Luxury...

Inside and out, this design speaks of space and luxury. Outside, cedar shake roofing contrasts nicely with the brick exterior to compliment arched windows and accent dormers. Double entry doors usher you into a two-story entrance with the staircase curving gently to second level rooms. Ten-foot ceilings throughout the lower level and nine-foot ceilings upstairs add to the spaciousness already created by large rooms. And, look at these kitchen features — 60 sq. ft. of counter space, a 5 x 6 step-saving island cooking range, a desk area, a windowed eating nook, and nearby patio access.

First floor — 3,307 sq. ft.
Second floor — 837 sq. ft.
Garage — 646 sq. ft.
Porch and patios — 382 sq. ft.

Total living area — 4,144 sq. ft.

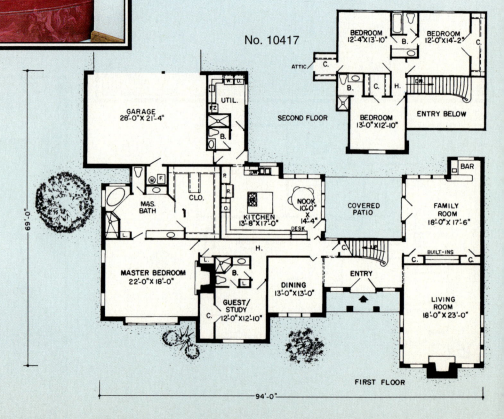

No. 10417

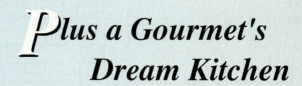

Plus a Gourmet's Dream Kitchen

No. 10417

Photography by John Ehrenclou

Beauty and character flow from every area of this design. The double entry, off set by brickwork arches, ushers you into a large foyer with a curving staircase. The family room and fireplaced living room have an abundance of windows and share a bar. The spacious kitchen has all the amenities of modern living, including plenty of counter space. In addition to the lower level master suite, three additional bedrooms are located upstairs and complete the sleeping accommodations. Each bedroom has direct access to a bath, and the largest of the three boasts a bay window and adjoining library. The photographed home was built in reverse.

First floor — 2,277 sq. ft.
Second floor — 851 sq. ft.
Garage — 493 sq. ft.

Total living area — 3,128 sq. ft.

*S*urround Yourself
With Beauty And Luxury

Photography by John Ehrenclou

Cozy Surroundings Sure To Please Everyone

Come into this spacious, welcoming foyer and step right into the Great room of this tastefully appointed home. The Great room is adjoined by a wrap-around deck and highlighted by a fireplace, built-in bookcases and wetbar. The first floor master suite is equally inviting with its spacious dressing area and separate bath. Adjacent to the central Great room, the kitchen area has its own built-in desk, octagonal morning room and central cooking island. The second floor includes three bedrooms linked by a balcony which overlooks the open foyer. The photographed home was built in reverse.

First floor — 2,419 sq. ft.
Second floor — 926 sq. ft.
Garage — 615 sq. ft.
Basement — 2,419 sq. ft.

Total living area — 3,345 sq. ft.

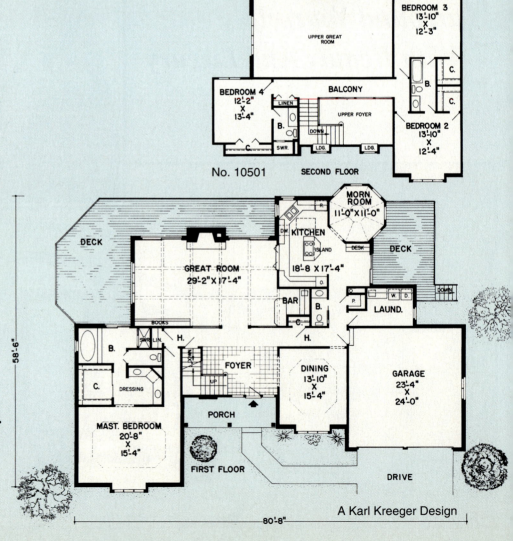

A Karl Kreeger Design

Photography by Charles Brooks Photographers

No. 10501

Luxury Design is Always Popular

A Karl Kreeger Design

No. 10531

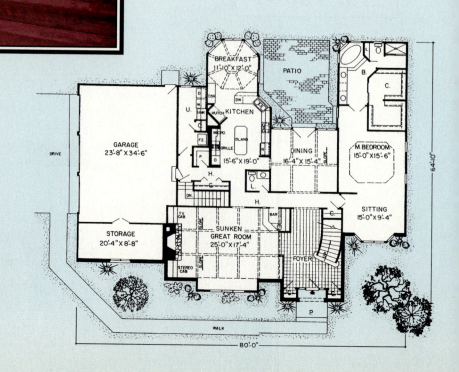

Here's a stately home that's a treasure chest of popular features, including a sunken Great room, a spectacular breakfast nook, and a bridge-like balcony on the second floor. The luxurious, first floor master suite is a marvel, with two huge walk-in closets, a 5-piece bath, and a sitting room with bay window. The second and third bedrooms each have a walk-in closet and private bath. The Great room features a bar, fireplace, and built-in cabinets for TV and stereo, all crowned by a sloping, beamed ceiling. Both the dining room and the foyer have cathedral ceilings and are overlooked by the seco/nd floor balcony. A fully equipped kitchen enjoys a sweeping view of the patio and opens to the stunning nook. All in all, this is a fabulous and impressive home.

First floor — 2,579 sq. ft.
Second floor — 997 sq. ft.
Basement — 2,579 sq. ft.
Garage & Storage — 1,001 sq. ft.

Total living area — 3,576 sq. ft.

Photography by John Ehrenclou

No. 10531

Photography by John Ehrenclou

*E*legant Touches Include A Morning Room and Hot Tub

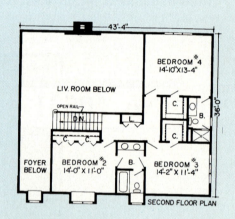

No. 10534

The luxurious master suite offers privacy on the first floor. Elegant touches include a library, morning room with built-ins; a bar with wine storage, and a sun porch with French doors leading into the dining room. The living room and foyer rise to the second floor which is comprised of three large bedrooms and two well-placed baths.

First floor — 2,486 sq. ft.
Second floor — 954 sq. ft.
Basement — 2,486 sq. ft.
Garage — 576 sq. ft.

Total living area — 3,440 sq. ft.

A Karl Kreeger Design

No. 10534

No. 10537

Four-Bedroom Design Appeals To Everyone

A Karl Kreeger Design

This roomy kitchen comes complete with a pantry and lots of cabinet space. The unique morning room is complemented with a large fireplace and an entry onto the patio for year 'round enjoyment. All four bedrooms are complete with baths and walk-in closets. The photographed home was built in reverse.

First floor — 3,114 sq. ft.
Second floor — 924 sq. ft.
Basement — 3,092 sq. ft.
Garage — 917 sq. ft.

Total living area — 4,038 sq. ft.

Photography by Alan McGee Photographers

Perfect For Parties...

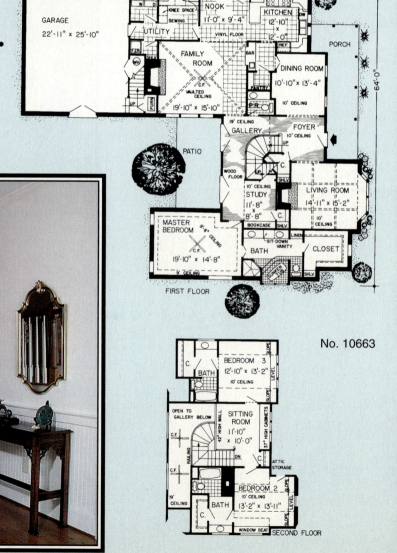

No. 10663

No. 10663

Does your family enjoy entertaining? Here's your home! This handsome, rambling beauty can handle a crowd of any size. Greet your guests in a beautiful foyer that opens to the cozy, bayed living room and elegant dining room with floor-to-ceiling windows. Show them the impressive two-story gallery and book-lined study, flooded with sunlight from atrium doors and clerestory windows. Or, gather around the fire in the vaulted family room. The bar connects to the efficient kitchen, just steps away from both nook and formal dining room. And, when the guests go home, you'll appreciate your luxurious first floor master suite and the cozy upstairs bedroom suites with adjoining sitting room.

First floor — 2,310 sq. ft.
Second floor — 866 sq. ft.
Garage — 679 sq. ft.

Total living area — 3,176 sq. ft.

Or For Relaxed Living

Photography by John Ehrenclou

Traditional Tudor Conveys a Warm Atmosphere

With its abundant windows and covered porch, this traditional Tudor masterpiece boasts an atmosphere that says "welcome". Show your guests into the sunken living room just off the entry, or the adjoining dining room at the rear of the house. With the efficient island kitchen just steps away, the cook's job will be easy. When the gathering's informal, the fireplaced Great room, which features access to both a screened porch and outdoor deck, is a comfortable alternative. Guests will appreciate the first floor powder room just around the corner. A graceful staircase leads to three ample bedrooms, each with a walk-in closet, one optional sitting room/bedroom, and two full baths.

First floor — 1,469 sq. ft.
Second floor — 1,241 sq. ft.
Garage — 3-car

Total living area — 2,710 sq. ft.

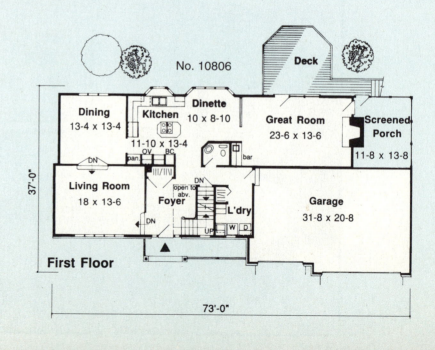

No. 10806

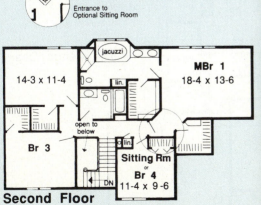

Photography by C. Strock Photographers

Angles Give Every Room An Interesting Shape

No. 34926

You'll never get bored with the rooms in this charming, three-bedroom Victorian. The angular plan gives every room an interesting shape. From the wrap-around veranda, the entry foyer leads through the living room and parlor, breaking them up without confining them, and giving each room an airy atmosphere. In the dining room, with its hexagonal recessed ceiling, you can enjoy your after-dinner coffee and watch the kids playing on the deck. Or, eat in the sunny breakfast room off the island kitchen where every wall has a window and every window has a different view. You'll love the master suite's bump-out windows, walk-in closets, and double sinks. The photographed home was built in reverse.

First floor — 1,409 sq. ft.
Second floor — 1,116 sq. ft.
Basement — 1,409 sq. ft.
Garage — 483 sq. ft.

Total living area — 2,525 sq. ft.

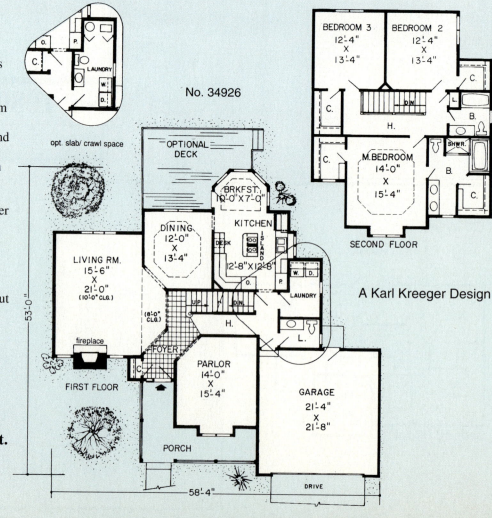

A Karl Kreeger Design

No. 10588

Two-Story Foyer Creates A Dramatic Impression

French doors in the breakfast nook give this traditional Colonial home a touch of romance. Divided from the kitchen by a peninsula with a counter for informal meals, the breakfast nook is adjacent to the fireplaced family room. Right across the hall the foyer links living and dining rooms and harbors the angular staircase to four bedrooms and two baths on the second floor.

First floor — 1,450 sq. ft.
Second floor — 1,082 sq. ft.
Basement — 1,340 sq. ft.
Garage — 572 sq. ft.

Total living area — 2,532 sq. ft.

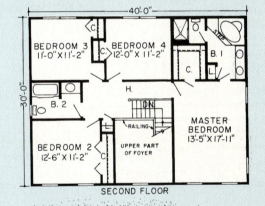

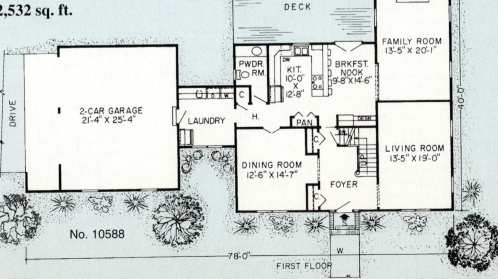

Detailed Charmer

No. 20161

Walk past the charming front porch, in through the foyer and you'll be struck by the exciting, spacious living room. It is complete with high sloping ceilings and a beautiful fireplace flanked by large windows. The large master bedroom shows off a full wall of closet space, its own private bath, and an extraordinary decorative ceiling. Just down the hall are two more bedrooms and another full bath. Take advantage of the accessibility off the foyer and turn one of these rooms into a private den or office space. The dining room provides a feast for your eyes with its decorative ceiling details, and a full slider out to the deck. Along with great counter space, the kitchen includes a double sink and an attractive bump-out window. The adjacent laundry room, optional expanded pantry, and a two-car garage make this Ranch a charmer.

Main living area — 1,307 sq. ft.
Basement — 1,298 sq. ft.
Garage — 462 sq. ft.

A Karl Kreeger Design

Total living area — 1,307 sq. ft.

Elegant Spacious Living

No. 20090

This expansive four bedroom Contemporary boasts balconies, skylights, and plenty of elegant details! Off the large foyer is the library/parlor with its wall of bookcases and high sloping ceilings. The formal dining room has a recessed ceiling, and provides accessible, distinctive entertaining space. Choose your kitchen option, and take advantage of the island counter. Enjoy the sunlit breakfast room and its full wall of windows, skylights, and a slider. The master bedroom suite, located on the first floor, features a large bath with whirlpool tub and shower, a spacious walk-in closet, and an elegant recessed ceiling. Upstairs, the balcony overlooks the substantial fireplaced living room below. Three good sized bedrooms share an airy skylit bath with double vanities.

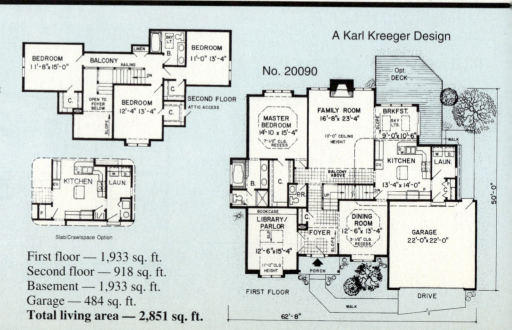

First floor — 1,933 sq. ft.
Second floor — 918 sq. ft.
Basement — 1,933 sq. ft.
Garage — 484 sq. ft.
Total living area — 2,851 sq. ft.

Many Treasures Await

No. 20179

Enjoy the impressive staircase as you enter the foyer of this home. The formal living room and dining room provide classic entertaining space. For a more contemporary gathering, take advantage of the roomy gourmet kitchen with its range-top island, and the open flow into the windowed breakfast area. Just over the railing the sunken hearth room awaits you. Take a step down and appreciate its well-designed sloping ceilings and space. Upstairs, find three large closeted bedrooms, a full bath, plus a master bedroom suite. This room features an elegant decorative ceiling, and an original bath and dressing room arrangement. Take full advantage of the whirlpool tub and double vanities.

First floor — 1,086 sq. ft.
Second floor — 1,057 sq. ft.
Basement — 881 sq. ft.
Garage — 484 sq. ft.

Total living area — 2,143 sq. ft.

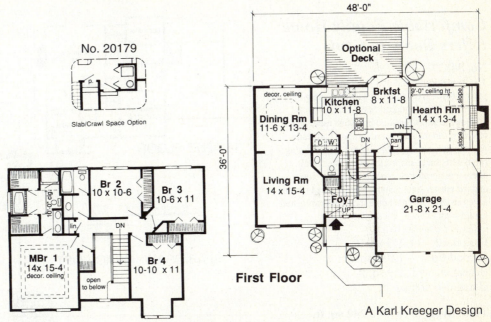

A Karl Kreeger Design

Comfortable Family Home Offers Room to Grow

No. 34827

The formal living and dining rooms off the central foyer greet your guests with a sunny welcome. The fireplaced family room beyond adjoins the bay-windowed breakfast room and has access to the rear patio. A short hall leads past the powder room, linking the formal dining room with the U-shaped kitchen. The three bedrooms upstairs each boast a walk-in closet and the master suite features both a raised tub and a step-in shower. This home includes an attached garage with two-way access and a large unfinished room above it.

First floor — 1,212 sq. ft.
Second floor — 1,030 sq. ft.
Basement — 1,219 sq. ft.
Garage — 506 sq. ft.

Total living area — 2,242 sq. ft.

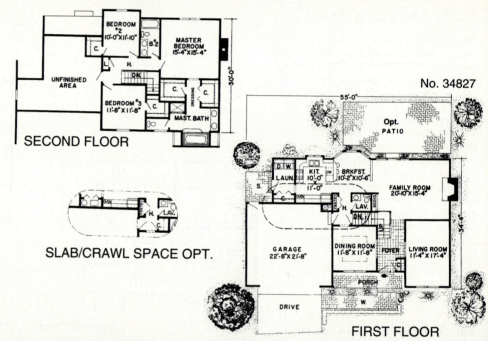

Traditional Energy-Saver

No. 20071

Take advantage of southern exposure and save on energy costs in this beautiful family Tudor. Heat is stored in the floor of the sunroom, adjoining the living and breakfast rooms. When the sun goes down, close the French doors and light a fire in the massive fireplace. State-of-the-art energy saving is not the only modern convenience in this house. You'll love the balcony overlooking the soaring two-story foyer and living room. In addition to providing great views, the balcony links the upstairs bedrooms. You're sure to enjoy the island kitchen, centrally located between formal and informal dining rooms. And, you'll never want to leave the luxurious master suite with its double vanities and step-up whirlpool.

First floor — 2,186 sq. ft.
Second floor — 983 sq. ft.
Basement — 2,186 sq. ft.
Garage — 704 sq. ft.

A Karl Kreeger Design

Total living area — 3,169 sq. ft.

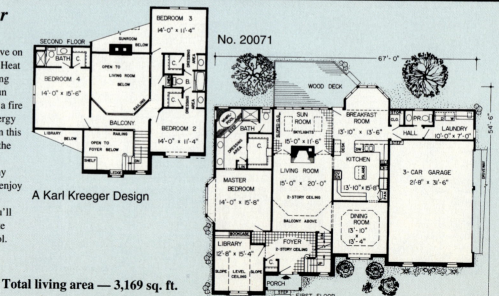

A Touch of Country

No. 10593

A charming porch shelters the entrance of this four bedroom home with a country kitchen. In colder climates, the closed vestibule cuts heat loss. Off the central foyer, the cozy living room shares a fireplace with the family room which contains a bar and access to the patio and screened porch for entertaining. The bay-windowed breakfast room is handy for quick meals or use the formal dining room with it's octagonal recessed ceiling. All the bedrooms, located on the second floor, have walk-in closets.

First floor — 1,450 sq. ft.
Second floor — 1,341 sq. ft.
Basement — 1,450 sq. ft.
Garage — 629 sq. ft.
Covered porch — 144 sq. ft.
Wood storage — 48 sq. ft.

Total living area — 2,791 sq. ft.

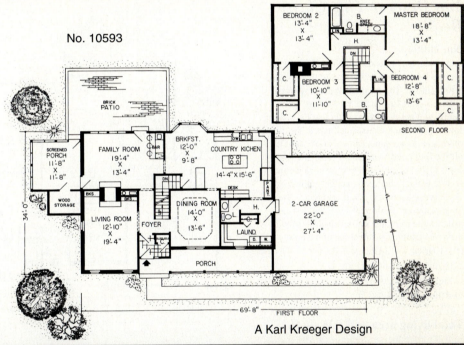

A Karl Kreeger Design

You Deserve This Classic Beauty

No. 20094

Sturdy stucco, fieldstone, and rough-hewn timbers lend a distinguished air to this updated Tudor classic. Inside, modern and traditional elements unite to create a masterpiece your family will never outgrow. Look at the soaring foyer, the elegant recessed ceilings in the dining room and master suite, and the book-lined library off the fireplaced living room. Imagine the convenience of an island kitchen with wetbar service to the living room, and an adjoining, skylit breakfast room. Think about how the three-and-a-half baths that serve the first-floor master suite and three upstairs bedrooms will make the morning rush a thing of the past.

First floor — 2,065 sq. ft.
Second floor — 970 sq. ft.
Basement — 2,047 sq. ft.
Garage — 524 sq. ft.

Total living area — 3,035 sq. ft.

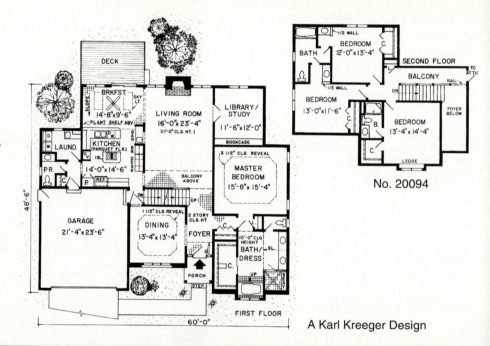

A Karl Kreeger Design

Decorative Detailing Adds Much Charm

No. 34005

The covered entrance of this classy home adds a touch of charm and elegance. The living room features a cozy fireplace set between two windows and a sloped ceiling. Off the living room is the kitchen equipped with a plant shelf, perfect for growing a fresh herb garden. A patio is accessible through sliding glass doors, providing a quiet escape from everyday life confusion. The dining room features a beautifully-designed ceiling enhancing formal occassions. Up a few stairs, past an octagonal window, is the sleeping wing. The master bedroom, also featuring a decorative ceiling, has a private bath and linen closet. A second bath is equipped with washer and dryer, located across the hall from the other two bedrooms. Please indicate crawl space or basement foundation when ordering.

Main living area — 1,441 sq. ft.
Garage — 2-car

Total living area — 1,441 sq. ft.

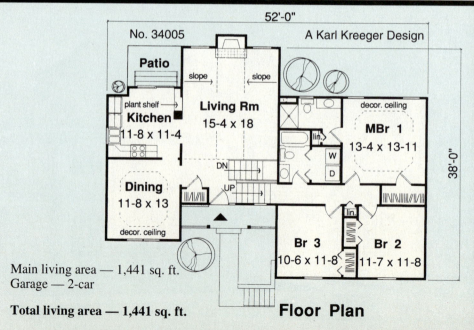

Floor Plan

Family Home Features
Private Bedroom Tower

No. 34049

Sloping ceilings and open spaces characterize this four-bedroom home. The dining room off the foyer adjoins the breakfast room and the convenient island kitchen. The beamed living room is crowned by a balcony overlook that links the upstairs bedrooms. The vaulted first-floor master suite features a private deck, a walk-in closet and a full bath with a double vanity.

First floor — 1,496 sq. ft.
Second floor — 520 sq. ft.
Basement — 1,487 sq. ft.
Garage — 424 sq. ft.

Total living area — 2,016 sq. ft.

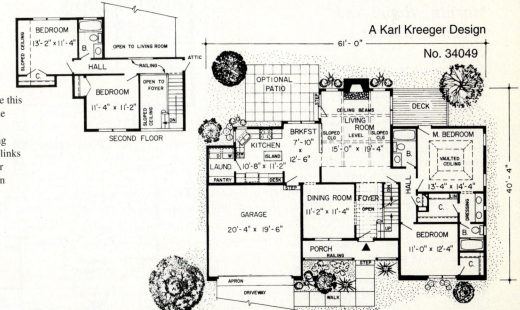

Morning Room Adds Gracious Accent

No. 10445

Tiled floors unify the dining and food preparation areas of this masterful design. Located off the well-organized kitchen is a morning room that's perfect for an elegant brunch or some private time before the day begins. Highlighted by a solarium, this octagonal room opens onto the centrally-located living room that features built-in bookcases, a fireplace, and a wetbar. The family room design employs more tile accents and opens onto the patio. The secluded master bedroom suite features a sunken tub, a small greenhouse for the plant enthusiast, and roomy closets.

Main living area — 2,466 sq. ft.
Garage — 482 sq. ft.

Total living area — 2,466 sq. ft.

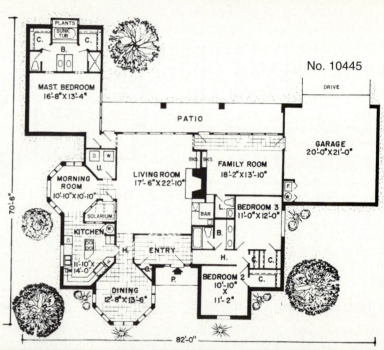

Tudor Grandeur

No. 20354

Gracious living is within your reach if you choose this updated, three-bedroom Tudor. Distinguished by an elegant, centuries-old facade of stucco and brick, sculptured roof lines, multi-pane transom windows, and a plan that uses every inch of space, this home affords its owners all the amenities of a larger house. A two-story foyer divides the main floor into formal and family areas. Notice the built-ins throughout: window seats in the living and dining rooms, the convenient range-top island and planters that separate the expansive family areas, and the handy bar tucked into a corner of the sunroom off the breakfast nook. Your houseplant collection on the ledge above the stairwell will add a greenhouse feeling to the second floor hall that links the spacious bedrooms and two well located baths.

First floor — 1,346 sq. ft.
Second floor — 1,196 sq. ft.
Basement — 1,346 sq. ft.
Garage — 840 sq. ft.

Total living area — 2,542 sq. ft.

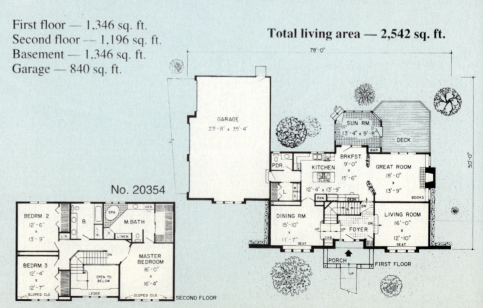

Charming Traditional Emphasizes Living Areas

No. 22014

In addition to its 20 ft. family room with fireplace, this one-story Traditional calls for a dining room, breakfast nook, and gameroom that can function as a formal living room if preferred. Each of the three bedrooms adjoins a full bath, with a master bedroom meriting a luxurious "his-and-hers" bath with two walk-in closets.

Main living area — 2,118 sq. ft.
Garage — 448 sq. ft.

Total living area — 2,118 sq. ft.

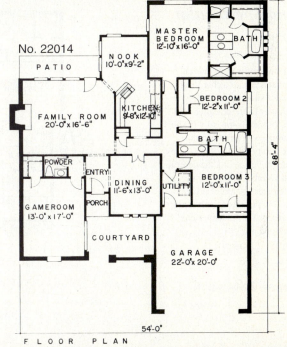

Secluded and Spectacular Bedroom

No. 10451

Create a secluded sanctuary for your master bedroom: a generous space with a charming fireplace, individual dressing rooms, and skylit bathing area. Relax away from the clutter and noise of the children's rooms, especially if you create a study or sewing room from bedroom two. You'll love the courtyard effect created by glassed-in living spaces overlooking the central covered patio with skylights. The sprawling charm of this house creates a sense of privacy everywhere you go. Extra touches, such as the wetbar and dual fireplaces for the family and living room, set this home apart.

Main living area — 2,864 sq. ft.
Garage — 607 sq. ft.

Total living area — 2,864 sq. ft.

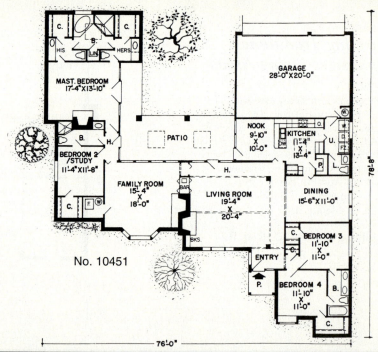

A Stately Home

No. 9332

This charming Traditional home retains the appeal of yesteryear, yet features an outstanding contemporary floor plan. Three large bedrooms each have a closet over seven feet long. The living room has a fireplace, square bay window, and ornamental iron railing which runs along the stairway and entry. A formal dining room opens onto an elevated wood deck through sliding glass doors. The huge family room, which also has a fireplace, is located on the lower level.

Upper level — 1,633 sq. ft.
Lower level — 858 sq. ft.
Garage & shop — 718 sq. ft.

Total living area — 2,491 sq. ft.

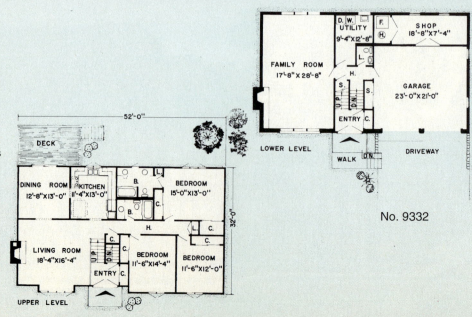

Roomy Four-Bedroom Brick Home

No. 22004

Four bedrooms, featuring a master bedroom with extra large bath, equip this plan for a large family or overnight guests. The centrally-located family room boasts a fireplace, wetbar, and access to the patio, and a dining room is provided for formal entertaining. An interesting kitchen and nook, as well as two and one-half baths, are featured.

Main living area — 2,070 sq. ft.
Garage — 474 sq. ft.

Total living area — 2,070 sq. ft.

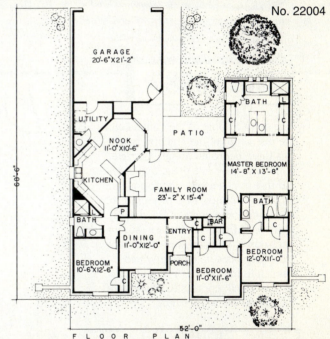

No. 10587

Designed For Entertaining

The double doors of the vaulted entry are just a hint of the graceful touches in this three-bedroom home. Curves soften the stairway, deck, and the huge bar that runs between the formal and informal dining areas. Skylights, bay and bump-out windows flood every room with light. And when the sun goes down, you can keep things cozy with fireplaces in the family and sunken living rooms. For a quiet retreat, sneak upstairs to the deck off the master bedroom suite.

First floor — 2,036 sq. ft.
Second floor — 1,554 sq. ft.
Garage — 533 sq. ft.

Total living area — 3,590 sq. ft.

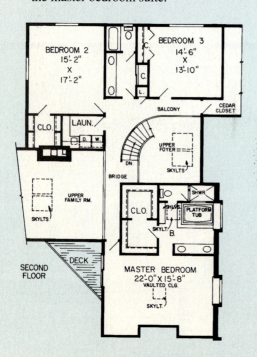

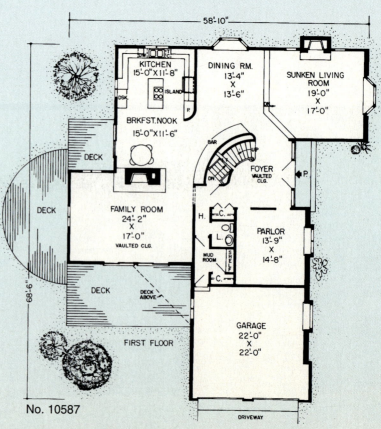

Fireplace Dominates Rustic Design

No. 90409

The ample porch of this charming home deserves a rocking chair, and there's room for two or three if you'd like. The front entry opens to an expansive Great room with a soaring cathedral ceiling. Flanked by the master suite and two bedrooms with a full bath, the Great room is separated from formal dining by a massive fireplace. The convenient galley kitchen adjoins a sunny breakfast nook, perfect for informal family dining.

This plan comes with either a basement, crawl space or slab foundation, please specify when ordering.

Main living area — 1,670 sq. ft.
Garage — 2-car

Total living area — 1,670 sq. ft.

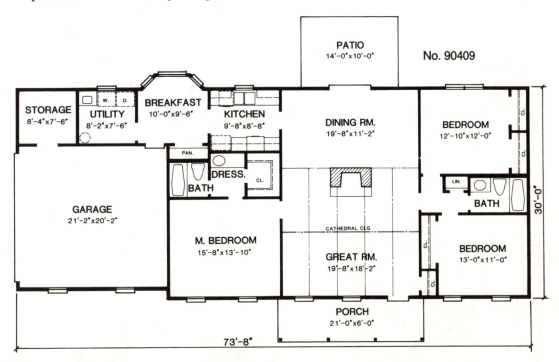

Porch Adorns Elegant Bay

No. 20093

Here's a compact Victorian charmer that unites tradition with today in a perfect combination. Imagine waking up in the roomy master suite with its romantic bay and full bath with double sinks. Two additional bedrooms, which feature huge closets, share the hall bath. The romance continues in the sunny breakfast room off the island kitchen, in the recessed ceilings of the formal dining room, and in the living room's cozy fireplace. Sun lovers will appreciate the sloping, skylit ceilings in the living room, and the rear deck accessible from both the kitchen and living room.

First floor — 1,027 sq. ft.
Second floor — 974 sq. ft.
Basement — 978 sq. ft.
Garage — 476 sq. ft.

Total living area — 2,001 sq. ft.

A Karl Kreeger Design
No. 20093

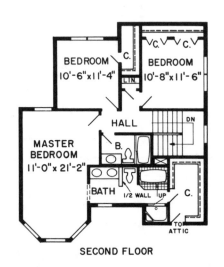

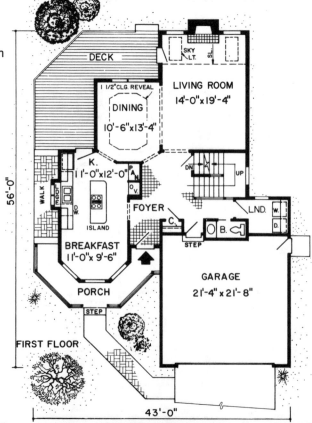

Balcony Affords Splendid View

No. 20097

Standing in the central foyer, you can see active areas and the rear deck off this sunny classic in one glance. Straight ahead, the living room ceiling, pierced by a skylight, soars to a two-story height. Living and dining rooms flow together in one spacious unit. And, both are easily served by the handy kitchen with a breakfast bar peninsula. Down a hallway off the living room, you'll find a quiet sleeping wing behind the garage. Two bedrooms feature access to an adjoining bath with double vanities. The second floor is all yours. Imagine stealing away for a luxurious soak in your private tub, or a relaxing afternoon with your favorite book.

First floor — 1,752 sq. ft.
Second floor — 897 sq. ft.
Basement — 1,752 sq. ft.
Garage — 531 sq. ft.

Total living area — 2,649 sq. ft.

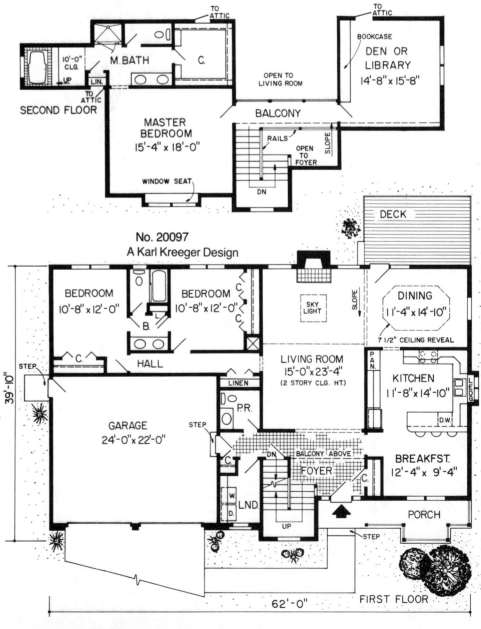

No. 20097
A Karl Kreeger Design

Exterior Promise of Luxury Fulfilled

No. 9998

Graceful Spanish arches and stately brick suggests the right attention to detail that is found inside this expansive three bedroom home. The plush master bedroom suite, a prime example, luxuriates in a lounge, a walk-in closet and a private bath. Exposed rustic beams and a cathedral ceiling heightens the formal living room, and an unusually large family room savors a wood-burning fireplace. In addition to the formal dining room, a kitchen with dinette and access to the terrace is planned.

Main living area — 2,333 sq. ft.
Basement — 2,333 sq. ft.
Garage — 559 sq. ft.

Total living area — 2,333 sq. ft.

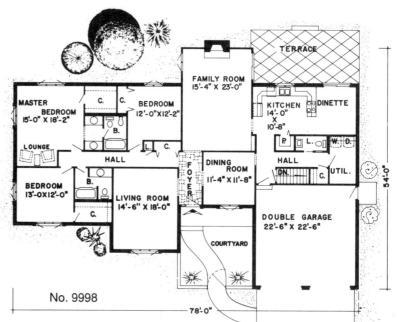

Home Recalls the South

No. 9850

Magnificent white columns, shutters, and small paned windows combine to create images of the antebellum South in this generously proportioned design. Inside, the opulent master bedroom suite, with plentiful closet space, a full bath and study, suggests modern luxury. Fireplaces enhance the formal living room and sizable family room, which skirts the lovely screened porch. The formal dining room boasts built-in china closets.

Main living area — 2,466 sq. ft.
Basement — 1,447 sq. ft.
Garage — 664 sq. ft.

Total living area — 2,466 sq. ft.

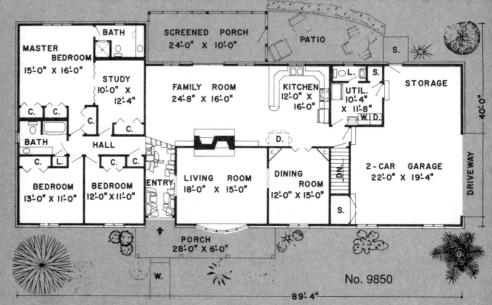

Sun Space Warms To Entertaining

No. 10495

Tile is used to soak up solar heat in the sun space and also to add a tailored accent to the total home arrangement. Leading from the air-lock entry toward the living room spaces of this marvelous home, the tile separates the activity areas from the sleeping quarters. With two bedrooms on the second story, the lower area includes the master bedroom suite with its divided bath and walk-in closet. The utilitarian areas of the home are also enhanced by direct access to the sun space plus a space-stretching central island.

First floor — 1,691 sq. ft.
Second floor — 512 sq. ft.
Garage — 484 sq. ft.
Sun space — 108 sq. ft.
Basement — 1,691 sq. ft.

Total living area — 2,203 sq. ft.

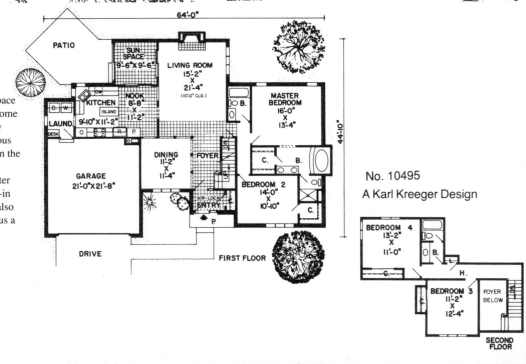

No. 10495
A Karl Kreeger Design

Family Favorite

No. 20156

The elegant half-round windows flanking the clapboard-faced chimney hint at the comfortable atmosphere you'll find inside this easy-care ranch. An open arrangement with the dining room combines with ten-foot ceilings to make the sunny living room seem even more spacious than its generous size. Glass on three sides overlooking the deck off the dining room adds an outdoor feeling to both rooms. And the compact kitchen, designed for efficiency, is just steps away. You'll appreciate the private location of the bedrooms, tucked away for a quiet atmosphere. The master suite is a special retreat, with its romantic window seat, compartmentalized bath and walk-in closet.

Basement — 1,359 sq. ft.
Garage — 501 sq. ft.

Total living area — 1,359 sq. ft.

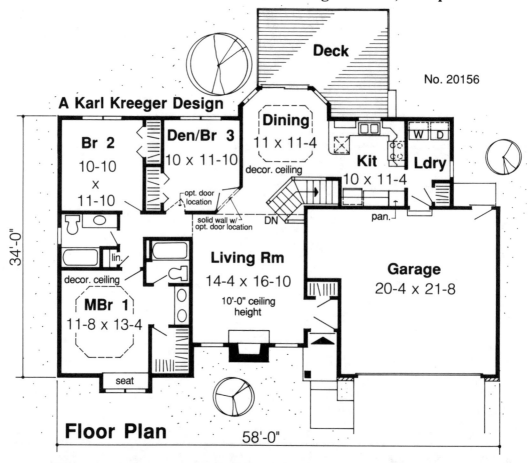

Skylight Brightens Master Bedroom

No. 34029

Keep dry during the rainy season under the covered porch entry way of this gorgeous home. A foyer separates the dining room with decorative ceiling from the breakfast area and kitchen. Off the kitchen, conveniently located, is the laundry room. The living room features a vaulted beamed ceiling and fireplace. Located between the living room and two bedrooms, both with large closets, is a full bath. On the other side of the living room is the master bedroom. The master bedroom not only has a decorative ceiling, but also a skylight above the entrance of its private bath. The double-vanitied bathroom features a large walk-in closet. For those who enjoy outdoor living, an optional deck is offered, accessable through sliding glass doors off of this wonderful master bedroom. Please indicate slab, crawl space or basement when ordering.

Main living area — 1,698 sq. ft.
Garage — 484 sq. ft.

Total living area — 1,698 sq. ft.

Slab/Crawlspace Option

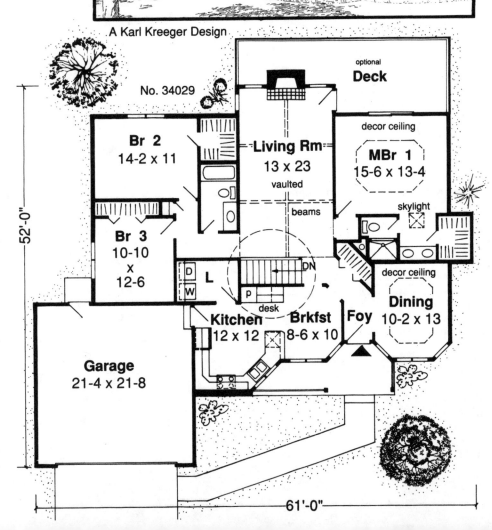

A Karl Kreeger Design

Angled Living Room Draws Attention

No. 10427

The exciting prospects of this home will satisfy those with an appreciation of beauty and design. Each area is singularly attractive as well as functioning with other rooms. Rising two stories to skylights above, an entry gallery routes traffic patterns to living and dining areas. The homemaker will find the step-saving kitchen a delight with its sunny corner sink, its location only steps away from the bay-windowed formal dining room, and the convenience of the nearby nook and pantry.

First floor — 2,300 sq. ft.
Second floor — 578 sq. ft.
Garage — 516 sq. ft.

Total living area — 2,878 sq. ft.

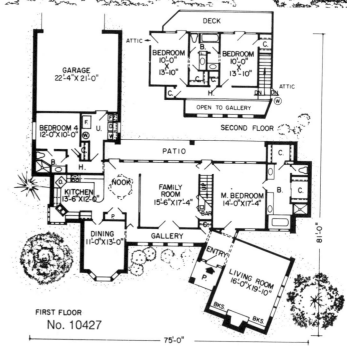

A Cape Cod Beauty

No. 9068

You'll love the way this beautiful Cape Cod home fits into your community. And, you'll appreciate the enduring value of this design. Note how every inch of space is used to good advantage in this plan. There are no costly offsets, and the rooms on the second floor have been made habitable by the addition of dormers, resulting in minimum construction costs. The exterior walls are frame, brick veneered. A full basement provides adequate storage or expansion.

First floor — 1,090 sq. ft.
Second floor — 652 sq. ft.
Basement — 1,090 sq. ft.

Total living area — 1,742 sq. ft.

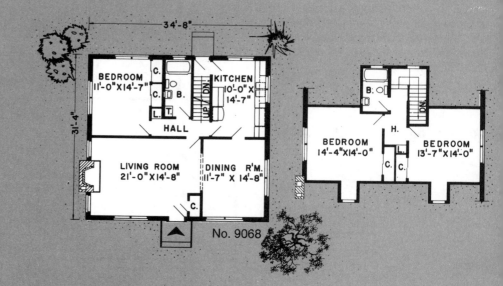

Entertaining is No Problem

No. 10610

Start picking out the porch furniture. You won't be able to resist sitting on this magnificent veranda on a lazy summer day. Walking through the front door, you'll encounter a large planter that divides the entry from active areas at the rear of the house. You'll find a sunny bay with built-in seating in the informal dining room, which shares a massive, two-way fireplace with the vaulted, sunken living room. If the living room bar doesn't fill all your entertaining needs, the nearby island kitchen certainly will. And, if the crowd gets too large, the full-length deck, accessible from the living room or breakfast room, can handle the overflow. There are two bedrooms, a full bath and a powder room on the first floor, but the master suite enjoys a private location at the top of the stairs.

First floor — 1,818 sq. ft.
Second floor — 528 sq. ft.
Basement — 1,818 sq. ft.
Garage — 576 sq. ft.

Total living area — 2,346 sq. ft.

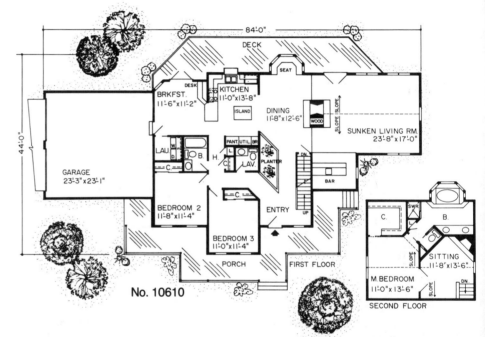

Romantic Porch Mirrors Dining Bay

No. 20124

You'll love the sunny atmosphere inside this distinctive, four-bedroom home. Bay and bump-out windows, sliders and skylights add light and space to every room, creating a pleasing unity with the great outdoors. Formal living and dining rooms flank the attractive entry foyer. Conveniently located at the center of the house, the island-kitchen is a cook's dream, serving all active areas with ease, including the deck off the hearth room. The first floor master suite features both a garden tub and step-in shower. Three more bedrooms, each featuring a walk-in closet, share a handy, double-vanitied bath.

First floor — 1,798 sq. ft.
Second floor — 879 sq. ft.
Basement — 1,789 sq. ft.
Garage — 484 sq. ft.

Total living area — 2,677 sq. ft.

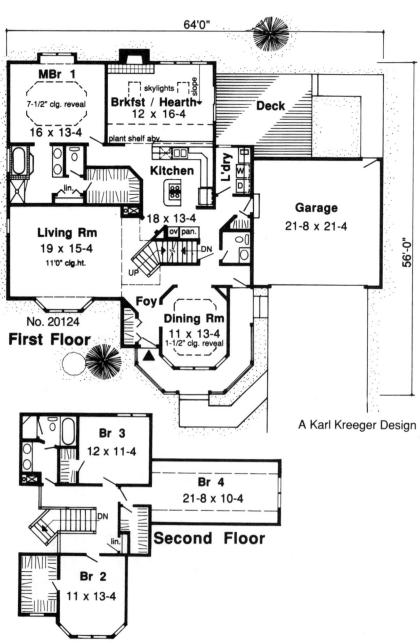

A Karl Kreeger Design

Cozy and Restful

No. 20195

The focus of this cozy home is on the first floor, but there is room for the children and their friends to gather in the lower-level family room which includes a fireplace and a powder room. The main floor features the living room, the dining room, the kitchen and a master bedroom with a decorative ceiling. There are also two additional bedrooms and a full bathroom with a skylight on the main floor. The washer and dryer are conveniently located outside the kitchen. The deck off the dining room can be used for outside eating if desired. This two-level is perfect for a hillside lot. This house is a cozy family retreat. The two-car garage has a lower level entrance.

Upper level — 1,139 sq. ft.
Lower level — 288 sq. ft.
Garage — 598 sq. ft.

Total living area — 1,427 sq. ft.

No. 20195

A Karl Kreeger Design

Cape Cod Passive Solar Design

No. 10386

A solar greenhouse on the south employs energy storage rods and water to capture the sun's warmth, thereby providing a sanctuary for plants and supplying a good percentage of the house's heat. Other southern windows are large and triple glazed for energy efficiency. From one of the bedrooms, on the second floor, you can look out through louvered shutters to the living room below, accented by a heat-circulating fireplace and a cathedral ceiling with three dormer windows which flood the room with light. On the lower level, sliding glass doors lead from the sitting area of the master bedroom suite to a private patio. Also on this level are a dining room, kitchen, mudroom, double garage with a large storage area, and another larger patio.

First floor — 1,164 sq. ft.
Second floor — 574 sq. ft.
Basement — 1,164 sq. ft.
Greenhouse — 238 sq. ft.
Garage & storage — 574 sq. ft.

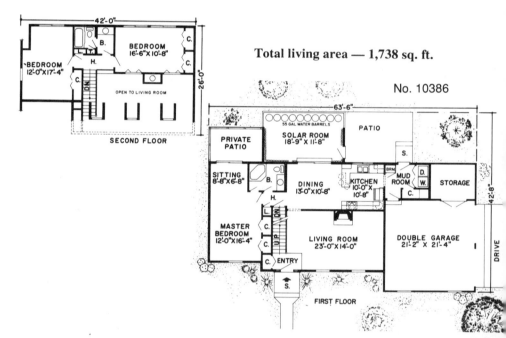

Total living area — 1,738 sq. ft.

Tasteful Elegance Aim of Design

No. 22020

With an exterior that expresses French Provincial charm, this single level design emphasizes elegance and offers a semi-circular dining area overlooking the patio. To pamper parents, the master bedroom annexes a long dressing area and private bath, while another bath serves the second and third bedrooms. A wood-burning fireplace furnishes the family room.

Main living Area — 1,772 sq. ft.
Garage — 469 sq. ft.

Total living area — 1,772 sq. ft.

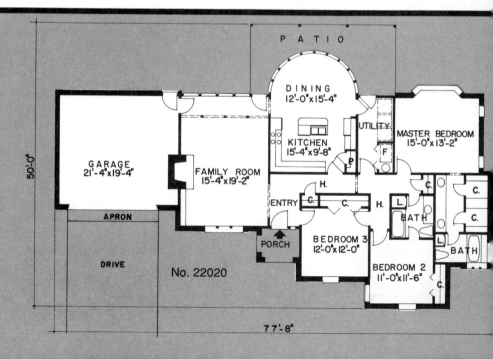

Timeless Elegance

No. 20105

The handsome Tudor exterior of this four-bedroom classic is mirrored by an exciting interior plan of extraordinary beauty. Step through the foyer, flanked by a formal dining room and library, and past the stairway to a massive living room characterized by high ceilings, abundant windows, and access to a private rear deck. With two-way access to the bar and fireplace, both living and hearth rooms share easy entertaining and a cozy atmosphere. The adjoining kitchen, with its handy breakfast bar and nearby pantry, is a marvel of convenience. Look at the recessed ceilings, twin walk-in closets, and luxurious bath in the first-floor master suite. Upstairs, three ample bedrooms enjoy walk-in closets and adjoining baths.

First floor — 2,080 sq. ft.
Second floor — 1,051 sq. ft.
Basement — 2,080 sq. ft.
Garage — 666 sq. ft.

Total living area — 3,131 sq. ft.

A Karl Kreeger Design

No. 20105

Covered Porch Offered in Farm-Type Traditional

No. 34901

This pleasant traditional design has a farmhouse flavor exterior that incorporates a covered porch and features a circle wood louver on its garage, giving this design a feeling of sturdiness. Inside, on the first level to the right of the foyer, is a formal dining room complete with a bay window, an elevated ceiling, and a corner china cabinet. To the left of the foyer is the living room with a wood-burning fireplace. The kitchen is connected to the breakfast room and there is also a room for the laundry facilities. A half-bath is also featured on the first floor. The second floor has three bedrooms. The master bedroom, on the second floor, has its own private bath and walk-in closet. The other two bedrooms share a full bath. A two-car garage is also added into this design.

First floor — 909 sq. ft.
Second floor — 854 sq. ft.
Basement — 899 sq. ft.
Garage — 491 sq. ft.

Total living area — 1,763 sq. ft.

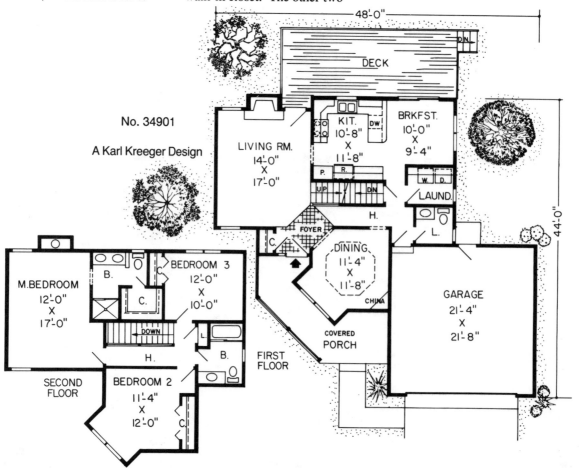

No. 34901

A Karl Kreeger Design

Enjoy a Crackling Fire on a Chilly Day

No. 10683

From the dramatic, two-story entry to the full-length deck off the massive Great room, this is a modern plan in a classic package. Cathedral ceilings soar over the formal dining and sunken living rooms, which are separated by an open railing. The corner kitchen efficiently serves formal and family eating areas. Can't you imagine a table overlooking the deck in the sunken Great room's sunny bay? Up the angular staircase, two bedrooms, each with a huge closet, share a full bath. You'll have your own private bath, including double vanities and a sun-washed raised tub, in the master suite at the rear of the house.

First floor — 990 sq. ft.
Second floor — 721 sq. ft.
Basement — 934 sq. ft.
Garage — 429 sq. ft.

Total living area — 1,711 sq. ft.

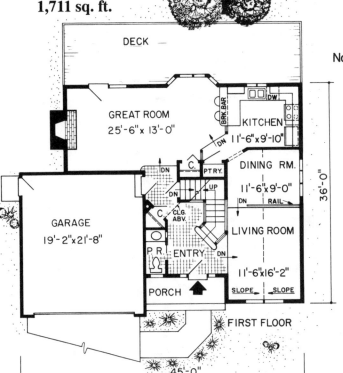

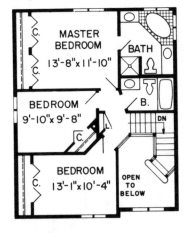

SECOND FLOOR

Classic Farmhouse

No. 10362

This house says "home" to everyone who remembers the bygone era but thinks ahead for comfort and values. The big wrapped-porch follows tradition. Imagine the cool summer evenings spent there. A split landing stairway leads to the four bedrooms on the upper level, complete with two bathrooms and lots of closets, perfect for the growing family. On the main level a wood-burning, built-in fireplace in the living room adds to the nostalgic charm of this home. Sliding glass doors open onto the porch. The main level also boasts a den, lavatory, utility room, kitchen and separate dining room overlooking the porch. An enclosed breezeway connects the double garage to the house.

Main level — 1,104 sq. ft.
Upper level — 1,124 sq. ft.
Basement — 1,080 sq. ft.
Garage — 528 sq. ft.

Total living area — 2,228 sq. ft.

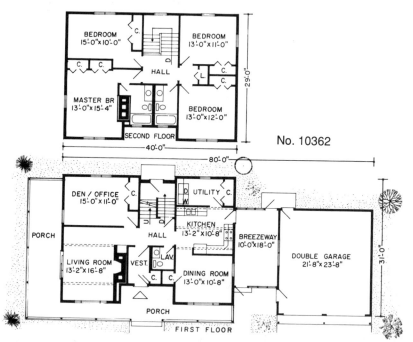

Dramatic Ranch

No. 20198

The exterior of this ranch home is all wood with interesting lines. More than an ordinary ranch home, it has a expansive feeling to drive up to. The large living area has a stone fireplace and decorative beams. The kitchen and dining room lead to an outside deck. The laundry room has a large pantry and is off the eating area. The master bedroom has a wonderful bathroom with a huge walk-in closet. In the front of the house there are two additional bedrooms with a bathroom. This house offers one-floor living and has nice big rooms.

Main living area — 1,792 sq. ft.
Basement — 864 sq. ft.
Garage — 928 sq. ft.

Total living area — 1,792 sq. ft.

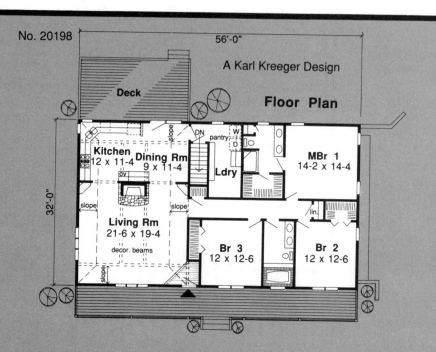

Entry Hints at Appealing Interior

No. 10678

Interesting angles give every room in this three-bedroom home a distinctive shape. Stand in the foyer and look up. Soaring ceilings in the window-walled living room rise to dizzying heights. Step past the powder room to find a fireplaced family room, wide open to the convenient kitchen with built-in desk and pantry. Just outside, there's lots of warm weather living space on the deck surrounding the dining room. Walk upstairs to the vaulted den that links the bedrooms and provides a comfortable spot for enjoying a good book. And, look at the adjoining deck! Can't you imagine perching up there on a sunny day, watching the world go by?

First floor — 1,375 sq. ft.
Second floor — 1,206 sq. ft.
Garage — 528 sq. ft.

Total living area — 2,581 sq. ft.

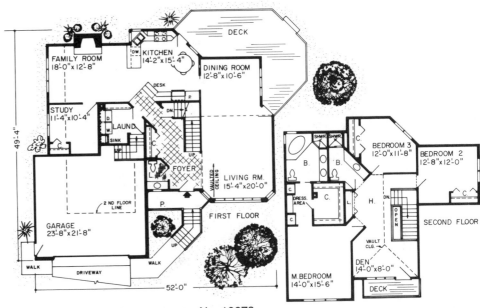

A Karl Kreeger Design   No. 10678

Two-Way Fireplace Warms Living Areas

No. 10652

Stucco, fieldstone, and rough-hewn timbers grace the elegant exterior of this three-bedroom family home. But with abundant windows, high ceilings, and an open plan, this cheerful abode is a far cry from the chilly tudor castle of long ago. Flanked by a vaulted formal dining room and a stairway to the upstairs bedrooms, full bath, and built-in cedar closet, the central foyer leads to a spacious living room, kept comfortable in any season by a ceiling fan. Nearby, the first-floor master suite is loaded with amenities: a walk-in closet, skylit double vanities, and a sunken tub. Notice the cook-top island convenience in the kitchen, the built-in bar adjacent to the living room, and the rear deck accessible through French doors in the breakfast room.

First floor — 1,789 sq. ft.
Second floor — 568 sq. ft.
Basement — 1,789 sq. ft.
Garage — 529 sq. ft.

Total living area — 2,357 sq. ft.

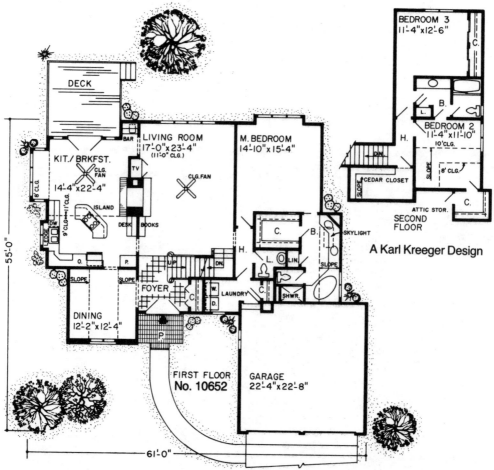

A Karl Kreeger Design

Perfect Compact Ranch

No. 10839

This ranch home features a large sunken Great room, centralized with a cozy fireplace. The master bedroom has an unforgettable bathroom with a super skylight. The huge three-car plus garage can include a work area for the family carpenter. In the center of this home a kitchen includes an eating nook for family gatherings. The porch at the rear of the house has easy access from the dining room. One other bedroom and a den, which can easily be converted to a bedroom, are on the opposite side of the house from the master bedroom.

First floor — 1,738 sq. ft.
Basement — 1,083 sq. ft.
Garage — 796 sq. ft.

Total living area — 1,738 sq. ft.

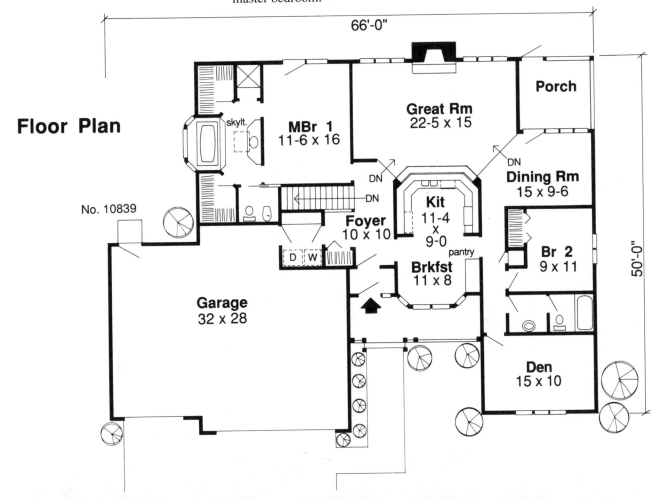

Floor Plan

Surround Yourself with Luxury

No. 10615

A magnificent home in every detail, this stately five bedroom residence surrounds you with thoughtful luxury. Enter the oversized, tiled foyer and view the grand staircase whose landing splits the ascent into separate wings and creates an aura of privacy for a guest or live-in relative in bedroom four. Serenity reigns throughout the home thanks to the courtyard plan that insulates the master bedroom complex and bedroom two from the main living areas. The kitchen is designed to serve the eating areas and family room and reserve the vast living room for more formal entertaining. Most of the home shares access to, and wonderful views of, the patio, covered by the second floor deck, and pool area.

First floor — 4,075 sq. ft.
Second floor — 1,179 sq. ft.
Garage — 633 sq. ft.

Total living area — 5,254 sq. ft.

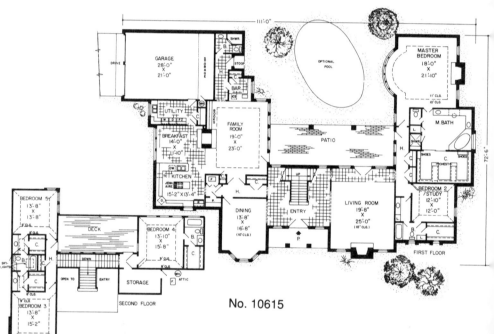

Attractive Entry Created By Plant Ledge

No. 10438

Dormers, decorative gable vents and bay windows balance on either side of the front entrance to give the exterior facade a look of symmetry. Inside, a planter ledge is found above the entry, lit by the two dormers and accessed through a bedroom for plant care. Raised hearth fireplaces found in both the master bedroom and living room, share a chimney. Two skylights illuminate the master bath and all areas on the second floor.

First floor — 1,454 sq. ft.
Second floor — 1,270 sq. ft.

Total living area — 2,724 sq. ft.

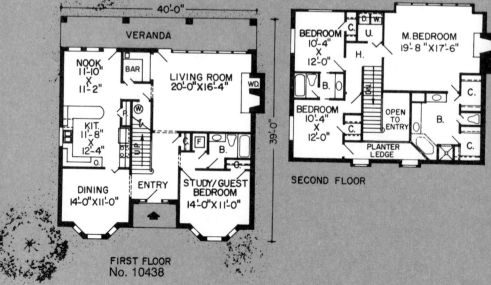

Skylit Loft Crowns Updated Traditional

No. 10754

Touches of old and new unite to make this a perfect home for the modern family. Rough-hewn beams adorn 11-foot ceilings in the fireplaced living room, mirroring the classic Tudor exterior. Elegant, recessed ceilings grace the master suite and formal dining room. Energy-saving fans lend an old-fashioned air to these lovely rooms. But, the modern plan brings efficiency to the huge island kitchen, which serves the dining room, breakfast nook, and adjacent deck with ease. And, the first-floor master suite, with its double vanities, walk-in closets, and luxurious whirlpool tub, is a convenient feature you're sure to appreciate. Tucked upstairs, two additional bedrooms adjoin a full bath.

First floor — 1,962 sq. ft.
Second floor — 870 sq. ft.
Garage — 611 sq. ft.

Total living area — 2,832 sq. ft.

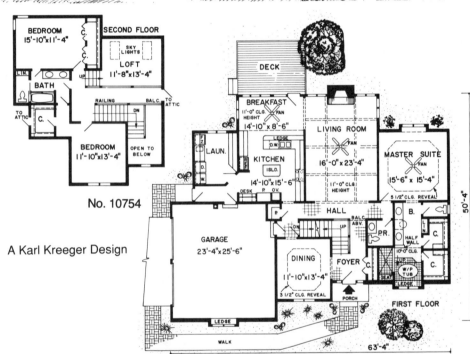

No. 10754

A Karl Kreeger Design

Six Fireplaces
No. 99215

Three wonderful floors of living space include a useful guest bedroom and study or hobbies room on the top floor. The second-floor master suite has a pampering bath. Three family bedrooms share a full bath on this floor as well. Living areas include formal living and dining rooms, country kitchen and library. Notice that this plan sports six fireplaces.

First floor — 1,656 sq. ft.
Second floor — 1,440 sq. ft.
Third floor — 715 sq. ft.
Garage — 2-car

Total living area — 3,811 sq. ft.

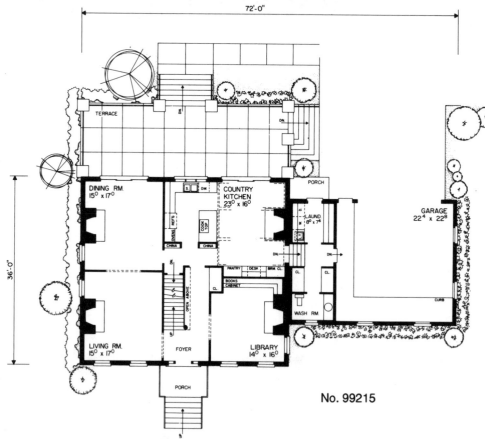

SECOND FLOOR

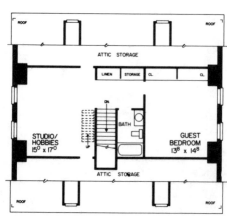

THIRD FLOOR

Romantic French Provincial

No. 90023

The romance of the French Provincial countryside is echoed in the exterior styling of this two-story, four-bedroom plan and should delight families with a taste for continental design. Its eye-catching character is derived from the curved window heads, angular bays, brick quoins at all corners of the brick veneer, steep roofs, and the diamond paned, copper-roofed picture bay over the double-door recessed entrance. The circular staircase with wrought-iron railing provides a luxurious access to the four bedrooms on the second floor. You'll enjoy the details which retain the good qualities and hospitality of an earlier era.

First floor — 1,900 sq. ft.
Second floor — 1,692 sq. ft.
Basement — 1,725 sq. ft.
Garage — 576 sq. ft.

Total living area — 3,592 sq. ft.

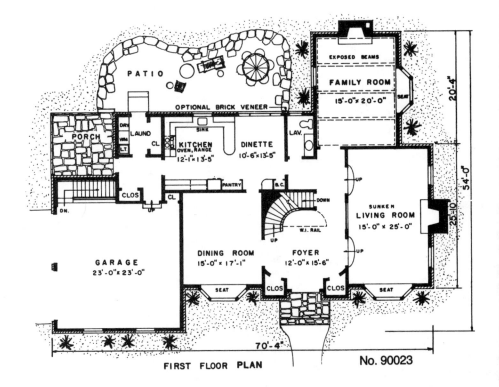

Covered Porch Provides Inviting Entry

No. 90419

With so many choices, you'll have a hard time deciding where to eat in this country Cape. Outdoor lovers will enjoy dinner on the deck, but formal dining or family suppers in the island kitchen are excellent options. The first floor location of the master bedroom makes one-level living a distinct possibility. But with a full bath and two bedrooms with cozy window seats upstairs, this wonderful home can provide room for many more. Please specify a basement, slab or crawl space foundation when ordering.

First floor — 1,318 sq. ft.
Second floor — 718 sq. ft.
Basement — 1,221 sq. ft.
Garage — 436 sq. ft.

Total living area — 2,036 sq. ft.

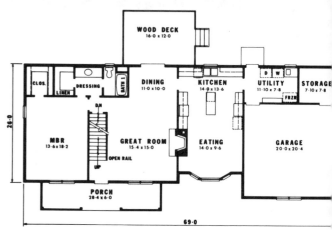

No. 90419

Classic Colonial

No. 90448

This classic Colonial can be built as a three or five bedroom home. The large Great room with a fireplace is located within the main part of the house. The formal dining room leads to a spacious kitchen, which is flanked by a breakfast room with bay window. Upstairs the master suite has a large walk-in closet, with corner tub and full-size shower, and double vanities. The two other large bedrooms share a second full bath to complete the second floor. The optional third floor includes two ample bedrooms with closets, and a third full bath. This plan is available with a basement or crawl space foundation. Please specify when ordering.

Main floor — 1,098 sq. ft.
Second floor — 1,064 sq. ft.
Basement — 1,084 sq. ft.
Unfinished third floor — 596 sq. ft.

Total living area — 2,162 sq. ft.

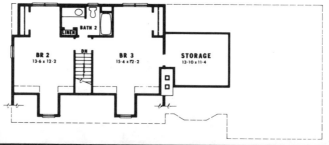

No. 90448

MATERIAL LIST AVAILABLE

Compact Victorian Ideal for Narrow Lot

No. 90406

This compact Victorian design incorporates four bedrooms and three full baths into a 30 foot wide home. The upstairs master suite features two closets, an oversized tub, and a sitting room with vaulted ceiling and bay window. Two additional bedrooms and a second full bath are included in the upper level. A fourth bedroom and third full bath on the main floor can serve as an in-law or guest suite. Between the dining and breakfast rooms is a galley kitchen. The dining room has a bay window and the breakfast room a utility nook. A large parlor with a raised-hearth fireplace completes the main floor. The porches add to the overall exterior appearances and help to protect the front and side entrances. Please specify a basement or crawl space foundation when ordering.

First floor — 954 sq. ft.
Second floor — 783 sq. ft.

Total living area — 1,737 sq. ft.

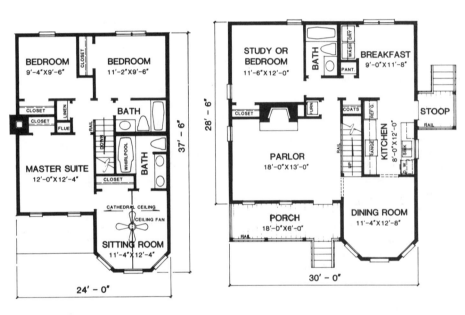

No. 90406

Classic Warmth
No. 10684

This compact traditional with clapboard exterior and inviting, sheltered entry boasts loads of features that make it a special home. Look at the built-in seat by the garage entry, the handy breakfast bar that separates the kitchen and family room, and the convenient powder room just off the foyer. Cathedral ceilings lend an airy quality to the living and dining rooms. A single step down keeps the two rooms seperate without compromising the open feeling that's so enjoyable. Sliders lead from both dining and family rooms to the rear patio, making it an excellent location for an outdoor party. Tucked upstairs, the three bedrooms include your own private master suite.

First floor — 940 sq. ft.
Second floor — 720 sq. ft.
Basement — 554 sq. ft.
Garage — 418 sq. ft.
Crawl space — 312 sq. ft.

Total living area — 1,660 sq. ft.

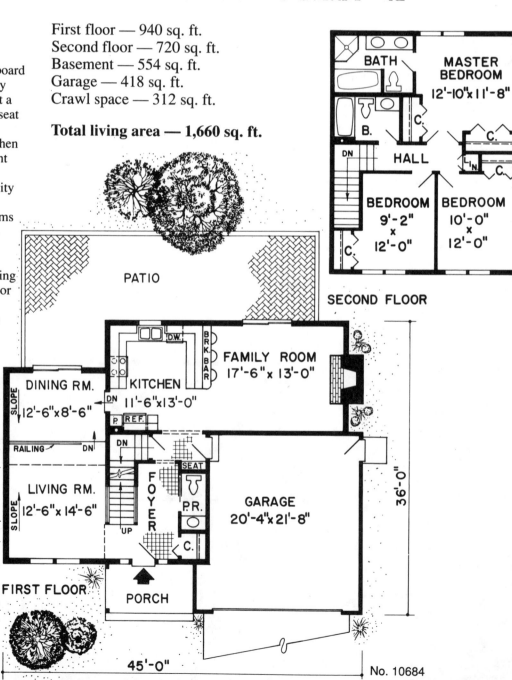

Two-Story Window Flanked By Stone Dominates Facade

No. 10494

The tiled foyer conveniently leads to the upper two bedrooms, the master bedroom, and the central living room. A corner built-in bookcase, fireplace and dramatic window wall complete this gracious room. The front dining room, enhanced by natural lighting, is convenient to the kitchen and adjacent breakfast nook.

First floor — 1,584 sq. ft.
Second floor — 599 sq. ft.
Basement — 1,584 sq. ft.
Garage — 514 sq. ft.

Total living area — 2,183 sq. ft.

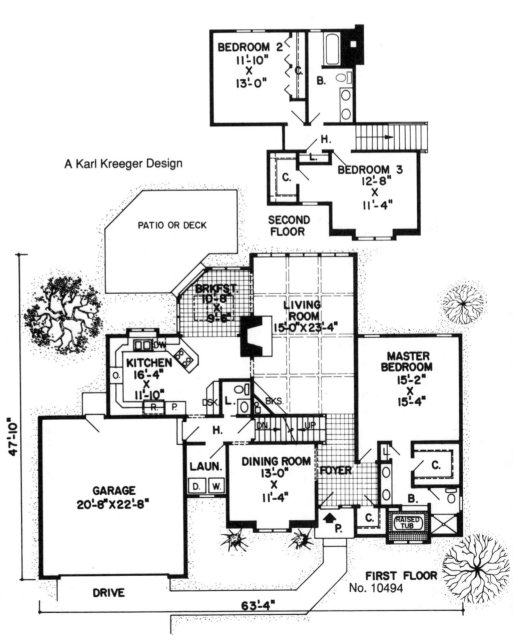

Room for Active Families

No. 10649

With two covered porches and a brick patio, this traditional Cape is an inviting abode for your outdoor-loving family. The central entry leads down a hallway to the family room. Warmed by a fireplace and boasting a wetbar, lots of windows and French doors, this enormous room is a great gathering place. Serve meals in the bay-windowed breakfast nook or the formal dining room located on either side of the kitchen. Window seats adorning the front bedrooms upstairs provide a pleasant retreat for quiet moments.

First floor — 1,285 sq. ft.
Second floor — 930 sq. ft.
Garage — 492 sq. ft.

Total living area — 2,215 sq. ft.

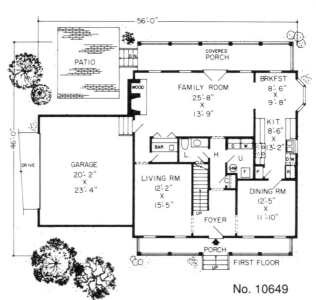

Exciting Ceilings

No. 20191

The uniquely shaped foyer leads into an elegant living room which includes a brick hearth fireplace and an eleven and a half foot ceiling. The dining room which flows into the kitchen has a decorative ceiling and overlooks the deck. One side of the house contains the two additional bedrooms which share a bathroom. The opposite side of the house contains a very private master bedroom suite with a decorative ceiling and huge walk in closet. The house also includes a two-car garage.

Main living area — 1,606 sq. ft.
Basement — 1,575 sq. ft.
Garage — 545 sq. ft.

Total living area — 1,606 sq. ft.

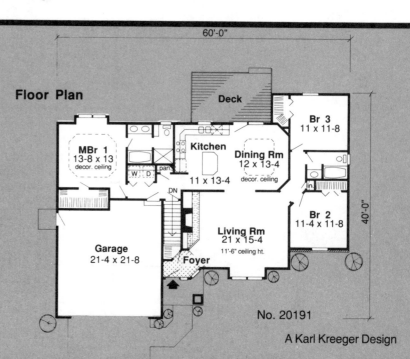

A Karl Kreeger Design

Easy Living

No. 20164

Here's a pretty, one-level home designed for carefree living. The central foyer divides active and quiet areas. Step back to a fireplaced living room with dramatic, towering ceilings and a panoramic view of the backyard. The adjoining dining room features a sloping ceiling crowned by a plant shelf, and sliders to an outdoor deck. Just across the counter, a handy, U-shaped kitchen features abundant cabinets, a window over the sink overlooking the deck, and a walk-in pantry. You'll find three bedrooms tucked off the foyer. Front bedrooms share a handy full bath, but the master suite boasts its own private bath with both shower and tub, a room-sized walk-in closet, and a bump-out window that adds light and space.

Main living area — 1,456 sq. ft.
Basement — 1,448 sq. ft.
Garage — 452 sq. ft.

Total living area — 1,456 sq. ft.

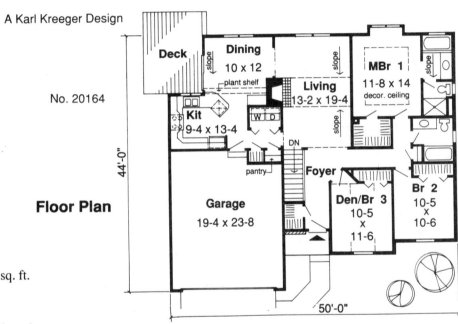

A Karl Kreeger Design

No. 20164

Floor Plan

Old-Fashioned Charm

No. 21124

An old-fashioned, homespun flavor has been created using lattice work, horizontal and vertical placement of wood siding, and full-length front and rear porches with turned wood columns and wood railings. The floor plan features an open living room, dining room and kitchen. A master suite finishes the first level. An additional bedroom and full bath are located upstairs. Here, also, is found a large bonus room which could serve a variety of family needs. Or it can be deleted altogether by adding a second floor balcony overlooking the living room below and allowing the living room ceilings to spaciously rise two full stories. Wood floors throughout the design add a final bit of country to the plan. No materials list available for this plan.

First floor — 835 sq. ft.
Second floor — 817 sq. ft.

Total living area — 1,652 sq. ft.

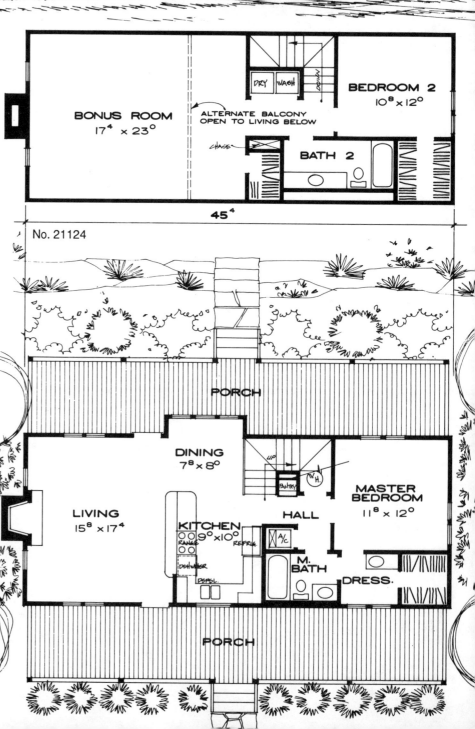

Warm and Inviting

No. 90827

Here's a traditional design for your growing family, complete with a rainy-day porch and a second-floor sitting area with a romantic balcony. The entry is flanked by a formal sunken living room and cozy family room. At mealtime, choose the formal dining room or the sunny, pleasant breakfast room off the kitchen. And, don't worry about tracking mud through your clean house. Deposit your boots and other items in the utility room by the back door. Three bedrooms, including the spacious master suite, share the second floor with the open sitting area and an adjoining study.

First floor — 1,349 sq. ft.
Second floor — 1,199 sq. ft.
Unfinished basement — 1,349 sq. ft.
Width — 57 ft.
Depth — 39 ft.

No. 90827

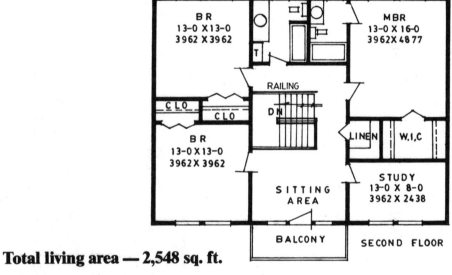

Total living area — 2,548 sq. ft.

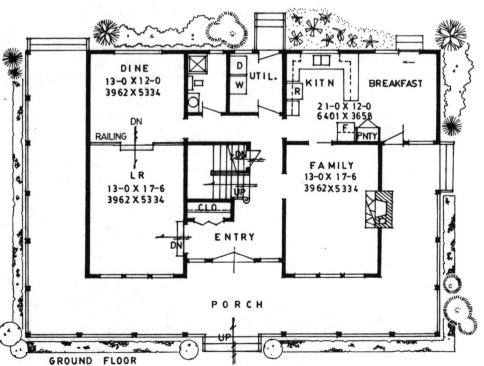

Windows are Highlights

No. 90118

Double windows in the living room and formal dining room, plus a bay window off the kitchen's dining area, enhance the livability of this spacious home. With your choice of four or five bedrooms, all located upstairs for privacy, individuality flourishes. There's even a mudroom conveniently located to the rear of the garage and adjacent to the kitchen for cleaning up after yard work. This plan is available with a basement foundation only.

First floor — 1,392 sq. ft.
Second floor — 1,282 sq. ft.
Garage — 2-car

Total living area — 2,674 sq. ft.

No. 90118

Family Living for the Budget Minded

No. 270

Two story efficiency and one story economy are combined to produce this roomy split foyer design. The rectangular shape assures minimum costs for maximum livable area. A large family can live peacefully in this home without stumbling over each other. The balcony at the rear, while not absolutely essential, provides an outdoor area for sun bathing or just relaxing to enjoy a cool evening breeze. The large garage provides storage space for bicycles, the lawn mower, etc.

Upper level — 1,456 sq. ft.
Lower level — 1,456 sq. ft.
Garage — 528 sq. ft.

Total living area — 2,912 sq. ft.

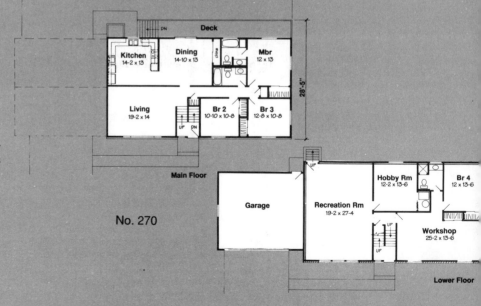

No. 270

Master Bedroom on First Level

No. 90142

This excellent traditional design has the master bedroom located on the first level and equipped with a walk-in closet and a large bath area that incorporates a skylight over the tub. Also on the first level is a living room with large bay windows allowing natural lighting to fill the room. The kitchen has an abundance of cabinet space and includes a pantry that has plenty of storage space. The laundry room is located just between the kitchen and garage. The second level has three bedrooms and one full bath. Please specify a basement or crawl space foundation when ordering.

First floor — 1,663 sq. ft.
Second floor — 727 sq. ft.
Garage — 2-car

Total living area — 2,390 sq. ft.

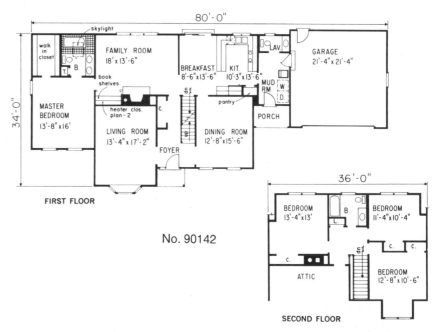

Everything You Need —Today & Tomorrow

No. 92009

This 2,307 sq. ft. two-story plan has everything todays move-up buyer wants, from it's covered country-style front porch with brick accents to the multiple front gables. As you enter the formal two-story entry you have access to both the formal living room and formal dining room, or proceed down the hall to large rear located family room with fireplace and corner glass. The large island kitchen features an eating bar to the family room, cooking island, a bright breakfast eating area with corner glass and sliding glass door to the rear deck. Upstairs the excitement continues with an open railing, to the entry hall below, leading to the master suite which features a large private luxury bath with plenty of closet space. Also upstairs you will find 3 additional bedrooms, laundry facilities, and a bath with double vanity and compartmented tub/toilet.

First floor — 1,059 sq. ft.
Second floor — 1,248 sq. ft.
Basement — 1,071 sq. ft.
Garage — 468 sq. ft.

Total living area — 2,307 sq. ft.

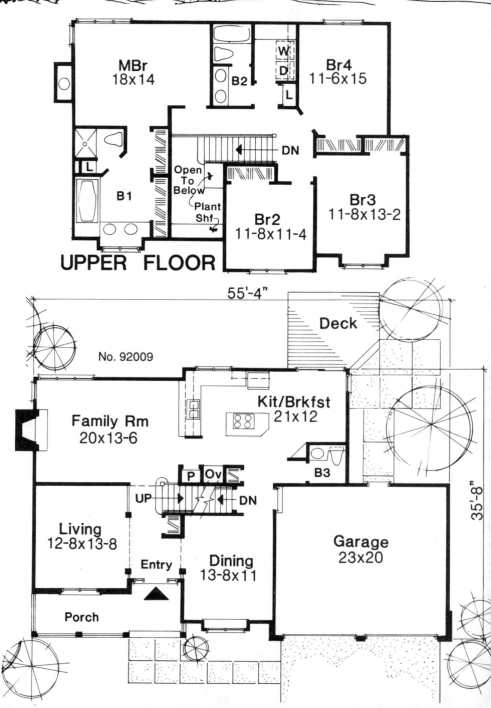

Classic Farmhouse With Elegant Amenities

No. 99608

This two-story farmhouse projects a relaxed style. But, there is elegance in the decorative curved stairway of the roomy foyer and the living room terminated with an ornamental heat-circulating fireplace. A dining room, enhanced by a large bay window is located off the living room and leads through sliding glass doors to a covered porch. A secondary hall serving stairs to the basement and a powder room, connects the central foyer to the combined kitchen-family room. This room has a high sloped ceiling, a heat-circulating fireplace, bayed window space and sliding glass doors leading to a huge rear terrace. The second floor has four bedrooms with ample closet space and two large-sized baths

First floor — 1,269 sq. ft.
Second floor — 1,006 sq. ft.
Mudroom — 58 sq. ft.
Basement — 854 sq. ft.
Garage — 403 sq. ft

Total living area — 2,333 sq. ft.

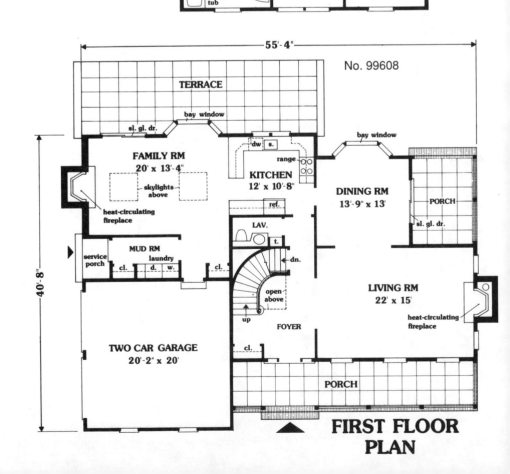

Home With A View

No. 10662

Here's a rambling classic that unites traditional elements with modern convenience. Columns adorn the entry and walled atrium. Stucco siding and a tile roof add to the classic beauty of the facade. With walls of windows in every room and French doors in the family room, you'll be able to enjoy your yard to its fullest advantage — even while you're inside. The huge cooktop island and central location make the kitchen a marvel of efficiency. And, you'll enjoy the first floor location of the master suite. Upstairs, double vanities in the full bath that adjoins the bedrooms make the morning rush easier.

First floor — 2,643 sq. ft.
Second floor — 927 sq. ft.
Garage — 1,170 sq. ft.

Total living area — 3,570 sq. ft.

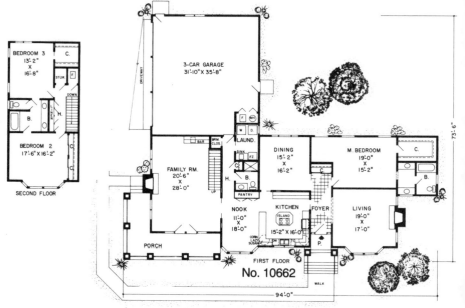

One-Floor Living

No. 20099

You'll find an appealing quality of open space in every room of this unique one-level home. Angular windows and recessed ceilings separate the two dining rooms from the adjoining island kitchen without compromising the airy feeling. A window-wall that flanks the fireplace in the soaring, skylit living room unites interior spaces with the outdoor deck. The sunny atmosphere continues in the master suite, with its bump-out window and double-vanitied bath, and in the two bedrooms off the foyer.

Main living area — 2,020 sq. ft.
Basement — 2,020 sq. ft.
Garage — 534 sq. ft.

Total living area — 2,020 sq. ft.

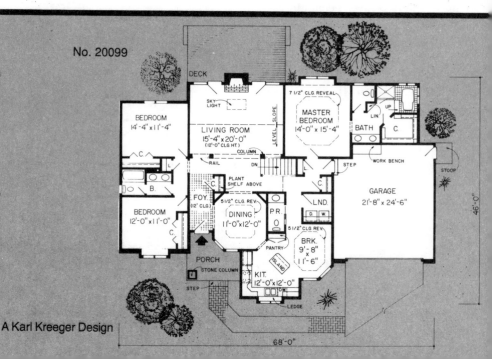

A Karl Kreeger Design

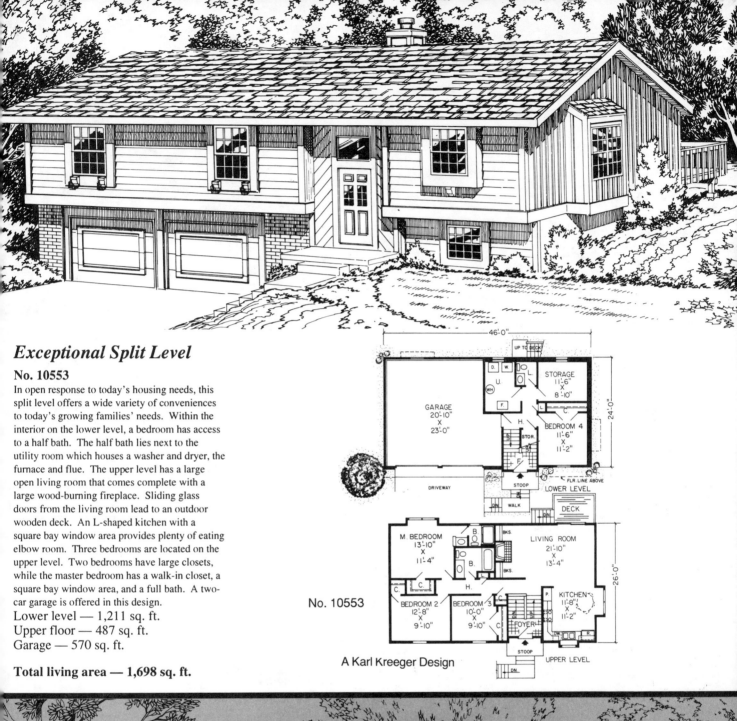

Exceptional Split Level

No. 10553

In open response to today's housing needs, this split level offers a wide variety of conveniences to today's growing families' needs. Within the interior on the lower level, a bedroom has access to a half bath. The half bath lies next to the utility room which houses a washer and dryer, the furnace and flue. The upper level has a large open living room that comes complete with a large wood-burning fireplace. Sliding glass doors from the living room lead to an outdoor wooden deck. An L-shaped kitchen with a square bay window area provides plenty of eating elbow room. Three bedrooms are located on the upper level. Two bedrooms have large closets, while the master bedroom has a walk-in closet, a square bay window area, and a full bath. A two-car garage is offered in this design.

Lower level — 1,211 sq. ft.
Upper floor — 487 sq. ft.
Garage — 570 sq. ft.

Total living area — 1,698 sq. ft.

No. 10553

A Karl Kreeger Design

Gingerbread Charm
No. 10690

Victorian elegance combines with a modern floor plan to make this a dream house without equal. A wrap-around porch and rear deck add lots of extra living space to the roomy first floor, which features a formal parlor and dining room just off the central entry. Informal areas at the rear of the house are wide-open for family interaction. Gather the crew around the fireplace in the family room, or make supper in the kitchen while you supervise the kids' homework in the sunwashed breakfast room. Three bedrooms, tucked upstairs for a quiet atmosphere, feature skylit baths. And, you'll love the five-sided sitting nook in your master suite, a perfect spot to relax after a luxurious bath in the sunken tub.

First floor — 1,260 sq. ft.
Second floor — 1,021 sq. ft.
Basement — 1,186 sq. ft.
Garage — 840 sq. ft.

Total living area — 2,281 sq. ft.

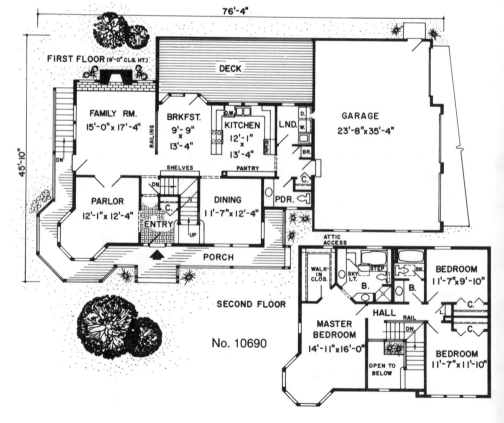

Country-Style For Today

No. 91700

No doubt about it, this plan, with it's wide wrap-around porch, matches the nostalgic image of a farmhouse. However, except for the living room, which can't help but remind us of an old-fashioned parlor with it's double doors, this house is thoroughly modern. High-ceilinged and bright, the kitchen, nook family room and dining room have a free-flowing lay-out and the area opens onto a wide deck. The first thing you see, upon entering the home, is the polished wood of a graceful open stairwell. At the second floor landing, it forms an open bridge. Two bedrooms are tucked away on the second floor with a full bath. The kitchen contains both a huge butcher-block work island and another long eating bar island. It also features a large walk-in pantry and built-in desk. The master suite has a spa and a huge walk-in closet as well as a shower, double vanities and its own access to the deck.

First floor — 1,785 sq. ft.
Second floor — 621 sq. ft.

Total living area — 2,406 sq. ft.

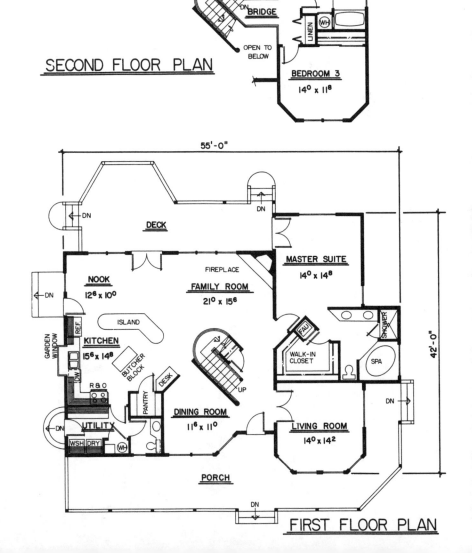

Classic Styling, Exceptional Plan

No. 90155

An appealing exterior is accented by the second floor overhang and gabled windows. A snack counter divides the U-shaped kitchen and breakfast area. Steps lead down from the kitchen into the sunken family room, which features a brick fireplace. A powder room and mudroom with entry from the garage allow for clean-up before entering the main living areas. The master suite is enhanced by a large walk-in closet and deluxe bath with corner deck tub and double vanity. Three additional bedrooms, two with walk-in closets, complete this exceptional layout. Please specify a basement, crawl or slab foundation when ordering.

First floor — 1,212 sq. ft.
Second floor — 1,160 sq. ft.

Total living area — 2,372 sq. ft.

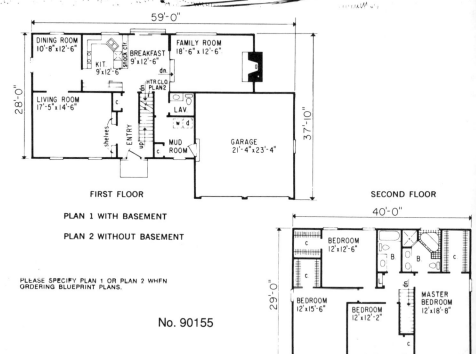

FIRST FLOOR
PLAN 1 WITH BASEMENT
PLAN 2 WITHOUT BASEMENT

PLEASE SPECIFY PLAN 1 OR PLAN 2 WHEN ORDERING BLUEPRINT PLANS.

SECOND FLOOR

No. 90155

Formal Balance

No. 20170

This lovely home combines classic materials and design to achieve a spacious feeling in a compact plan. The central entry, dominated by a straight staircase, divides formal and informal areas. You'll find an open breakfast room and kitchen combination to the left. And to the right, the formal dining room is just steps away from the sunny ambience of a fireplaced living room with sliders to a rear deck. A short hall offers access to a powder room, laundry room, and two-car garage. Upstairs, all four bedrooms feature large walk-in closets. A hall bath serves the kids' rooms. But the master suite, with its elegant vaulted-ceilings and bay windows, enjoys its own private bath with double vanities.

First floor — 914 sq. ft.
Second floor — 950 sq. ft.
Optional area — 241 sq. ft.
Garage — 528 sq. ft.

A Karl Kreeger Design

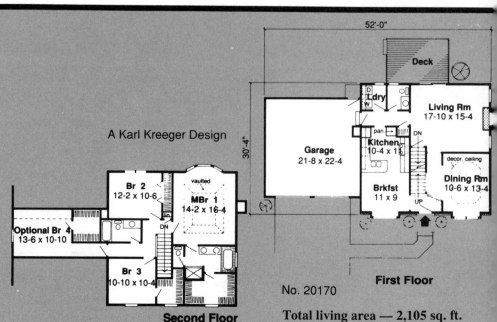

No. 20170

Total living area — 2,105 sq. ft.

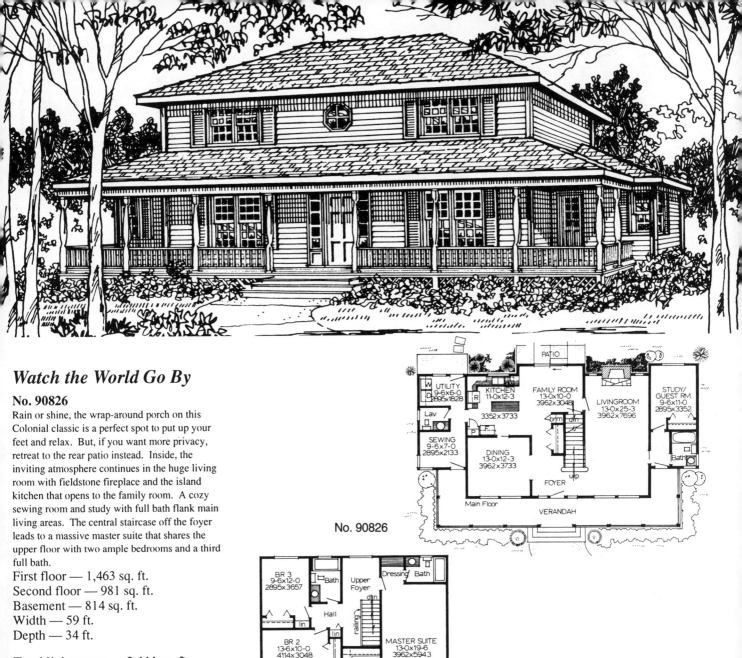

Watch the World Go By

No. 90826

Rain or shine, the wrap-around porch on this Colonial classic is a perfect spot to put up your feet and relax. But, if you want more privacy, retreat to the rear patio instead. Inside, the inviting atmosphere continues in the huge living room with fieldstone fireplace and the island kitchen that opens to the family room. A cozy sewing room and study with full bath flank main living areas. The central staircase off the foyer leads to a massive master suite that shares the upper floor with two ample bedrooms and a third full bath.

First floor — 1,463 sq. ft.
Second floor — 981 sq. ft.
Basement — 814 sq. ft.
Width — 59 ft.
Depth — 34 ft.

Total living area — 2,444 sq. ft.

Unique Rooms add Character

No. 99246

This home combines the best of ranch-style living with lots of luxurious space and special details. Consider the master suite: matching walk-in closets on either side of the dressing area, with a short walk to the whirlpool. The country kitchen has ample seating space in front of the open fireplace, a four-seat breakfast bar, and cooking area that lets you stay with your guests while you whip up a gourmet feast. The "clutter" room will become one of your most treasured spots — it has room for laundry, workbench and tool storage, center work island, sewing area and lots of storage cupboards.

Main living area — 2,758 sq. ft.
Greenhouse — 149 sq. ft.
Garage — 2-car
Basement — 2,758 sq. ft.

Total living area — 2,758 sq. ft.

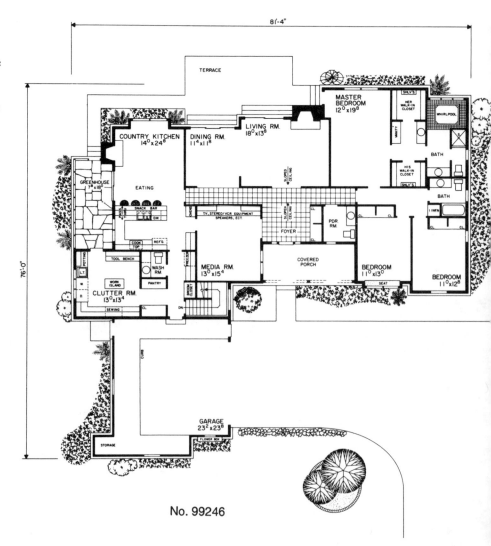

No. 99246

Master Retreat Crowns Spacious Home

No. 19422

Here's a compact beauty with a wide-open feeling. Step past the inviting front porch, and savor a breathtaking view of active areas: the columned entry with its open staircase and windows high overhead, the soaring living room, divided from the kitchen and dining room by the towering fireplace chimney, the screened porch beyond the triple living room windows. Tucked behind the stairs, you'll find a cozy parlor. And, across the hall, a bedroom with an adjoining full bath features access to the screened porch. Upstairs, the master suite is an elegant retreat you'll want to come home for, with its romantic dormer window seat, private balcony, and double-vanitied bath.

First floor — 1,290 sq. ft.
Second floor — 405 sq. ft.
Screened porch — 152 sq. ft.
Garage — 513 sq. ft.

Total living area — 1,695 sq. ft.

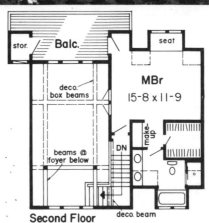

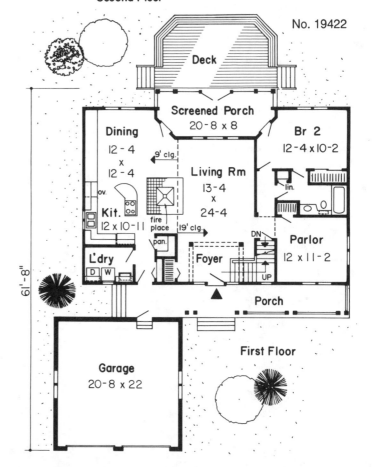

Compact Plan Allows For Gracious Living

No. 90158

A Great room, accessible from the foyer, offers a cathedral ceiling with exposed beams, brick fireplace, and access to the rear patio. The kitchen/breakfast area with center island is accented by the round-top window. The master bedroom has a full bath and walk-in closet. Two additional bedrooms and bath help make this an ideal plan for any growing family. Please specify a basement, slab or crawl space foundation when ordering.

Main living area — 1,540 sq. ft.
Basement — 1,540 sq. ft.
Garage — 2-car

Total living area — 1,540 sq. ft.

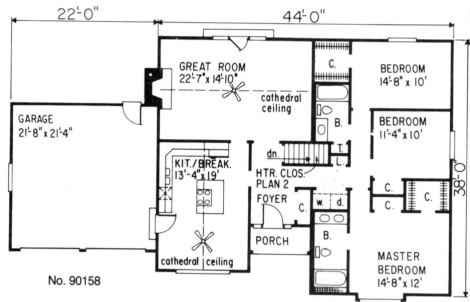

Touched with Tudor

No. 20088

A Karl Kreeger Design

Here's an elegant home for your growing family. With four upstairs bedrooms, each featuring a walk-in closet, there's plenty of room for everyone. And, three full baths insure the morning rush won't be a problem. Down the U-shaped stairway, a central hallway links family areas at the rear of the house with the two-story foyer and formal areas. Living and dining rooms, featuring a bump-out window and recessed ceiling, form one open space. With the island kitchen right next door, entertaining will be easy. Enjoy family meals in the breakfast room with adjoining pantry, or out on the deck. Window walls and sliders in the breakfast room and fireplaced family room unite outdoor and interior spaces for an airy feeling your family will cherish.

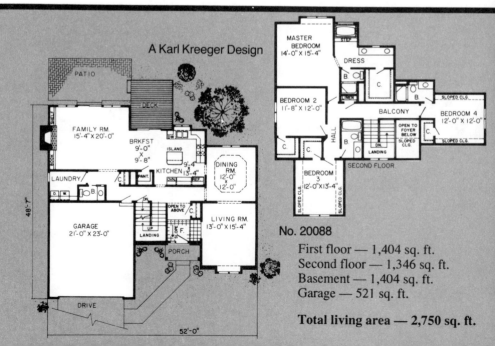

First floor — 1,404 sq. ft.
Second floor — 1,346 sq. ft.
Basement — 1,404 sq. ft.
Garage — 521 sq. ft.

Total living area — 2,750 sq. ft.

Sunny Split

No. 90950

Here's a unique approach to the split-level home. A central, glass-walled foyer creates a brilliant impression on all who enter. Walk down to the fireplaced family room, double garage with workbench, a very private bedroom, full bath and utility area. Main living areas are situated for comfort and convenience. In the bedroom wing to the right of the open staircase, a skylit hall bath serves the two front bedrooms. The master suite enjoys a backyard view and private bath with mirrored dressing room. Active areas possess a wonderful, open atmosphere accented by a huge bay window in the living room and sliders in the dining room and informal nook that flank the kitchen. The sundeck is a great dining option when the weather's nice.

Upper floor — 1,473 sq. ft.
Lower floor — 791 sq. ft.
Garage — 2-car

Total living area — 2,264 sq. ft.

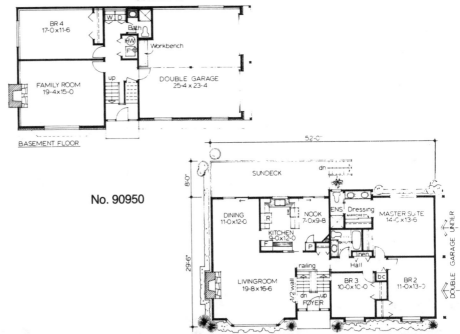

No. 90950

Nostalgia Returns

No. 99321

The return to nostalgic exterior envelopes around contemporary volumetric interior spaces of the late 80's is reflected in this appealing 1,368 square foot ranch design. The half-round Great room transom window with quarter round detail makes for an interesting focal point inside and out. The vaulted ceilings inside make the rooms feel spacious, while the corner fireplace and side deck through the breakfast room sliders create an interesting entry impact.

Main floor — 1,368 sq. ft.
Garage — 2-car

Total living area — 1,368 sq. ft.

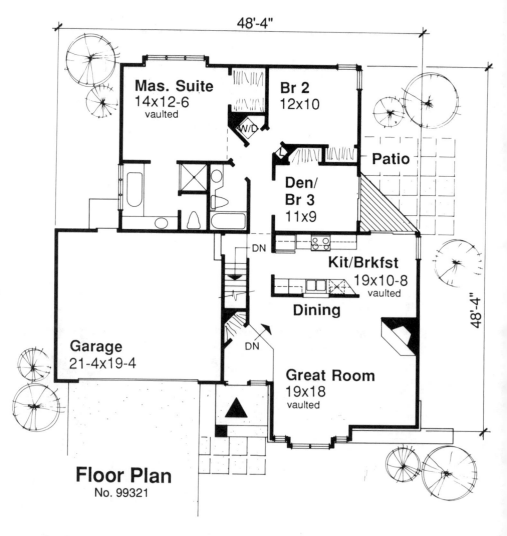

Floor Plan
No. 99321

Country Comfort

No. 91204

Imagine backyard barbecues on the rear deck off this rambling ranch house. The handy kitchen pass-through will insure that serving the side dishes will be a simple matter. You'll love the convenience of the eat-in country kitchen off the foyer. Want a formal atmosphere? Close off the bustle of mealtime preparation with sliding panels. And, after supper, put up your feet, sit by the fire and enjoy the airy atmosphere that soaring ceilings and sliding glass doors give the sunken Great room. Three bedrooms are tucked away from active areas. Look at the master suite. Even the largest wardrobe will fit in those twin walk-in closets!

Main living area — 1,974 sq. ft.
Garage and storage — 612 sq. ft.

Total living area — 1,974 sq. ft.

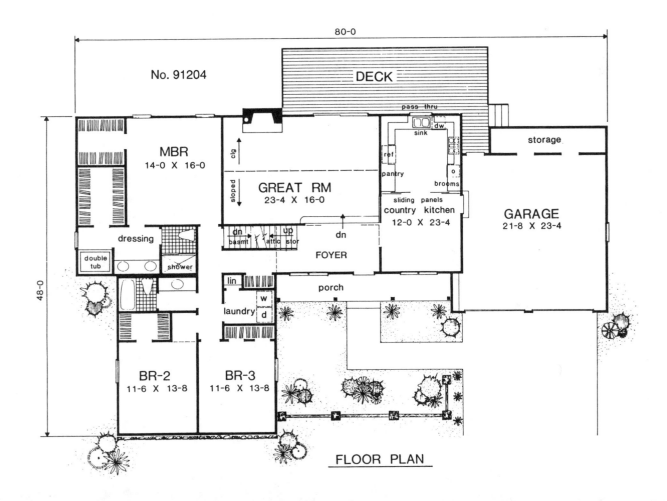

FLOOR PLAN

Four Bedroom Charmer

No. 91346

Abounding with amenities, this single level ranch home has an attractive street appearance with brick accents on cedar siding. A vaulted naturally lighted entry opens to a vaulted living room featuring a masonry fireplace, large windowed bay. The connecting dining room has a coffered ceiling and built-in china storage. To the rear of the house is a large vaulted family room with wood stove alcove, rear deck cooking island, large pantry and a telephone desk. A unique skylighted hall leads to the bedroom wing, consisting of two secondary bedrooms sharing a full bath. The luxurious master bedroom suite has a whirlpool garden tub, walk-in closet and double sink vanity. Completing this wing, is an abundant storage utility room. Hall access is provided to the three-car garage. Off the entry hall, is a study with window seat and built-in book shelves. This room can be used as a fourth bedroom.

Main living area — 2,185 sq. ft.
Garage — 3-car

Total living area — 2,185 sq. ft.

Railing Divides Living Spaces

No. 10596

This one-level design is a celebration of light and open space. From the foyer, view the dining room, island kitchen, breakfast room, living room, and outdoor deck in one sweeping glance. Bay windows add pleasing angles and lots of sunshine to eating areas and the master suite. And, a wall of windows brings the outdoors into the two back bedrooms.

Main living area — 1,740 sq. ft.
Basement — 1,377 sq. ft.
Garage — 480 sq. ft.

Total living area — 1,740 sq. ft.

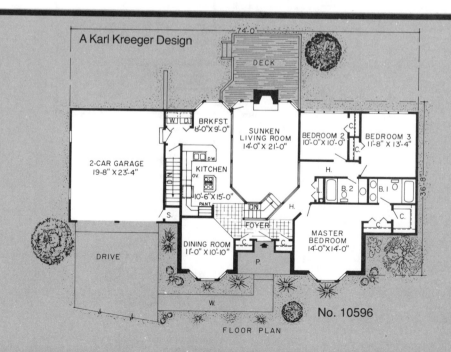

Charming Traditional Design

No. 10572

Warm features abound in this attractive traditional design. The exterior has a stucco and brick facade with a wood shake shingle roof and wood veneer siding on its side and rear elevations. Excellent traffic patterns exist on the first floor. Three bedrooms are located to the left of the foyer. Additionally on the first floor, the master bedroom has a walk-in closet and its own full bath. Two other bedrooms share a full bath. Straight ahead of the foyer is a spacious Great room with a beautiful open-beamed ceiling and at the end of the Great room is a large wood-burning fireplace with built-in bookshelves located on both sides of the fireplace. To the right of the foyer is the dining room with an elevated ceiling and a bay window.

First floor — 2,022 sq. ft.
Dormer plan — 354 sq. ft.
Basement — 1,980 sq. ft.
Garage — 526 sq. ft.

Total living area — 2,376 sq. ft.

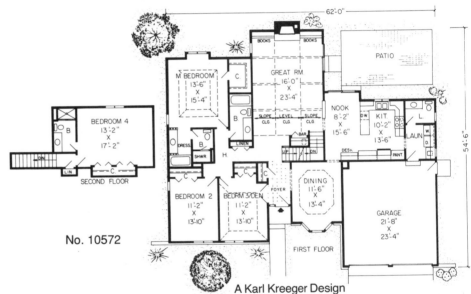

No. 10572

A Karl Kreeger Design

Empty Nester

No. 99360

The majority of living is done on the one level of this three bedroom, 1-1/2-story home. The entry, being open to the second floor, gives a feeling of space. Walk on into the fireplaced family room, a great place for the family to relax or entertain. The bay windows in the breakfast nook give a sunny start to your day. The step-in pantry off the kitchen offers plenty of storage space. Secondary bedrooms are located upstairs for added privacy. The master suite has a vaulted ceiling, its own bath and walk-in closet space. For a formal dinner party, your home has vaulted dining and living rooms that access each other.

First floor — 1,538 sq. ft.
Second floor — 465 sq. ft.
Garage — 2-car

Total living area — 2,003 sq. ft.

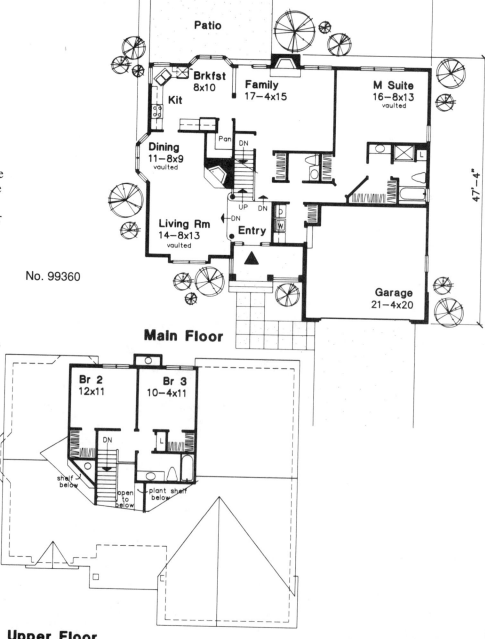

No. 99360

Main Floor

Upper Floor

For the Growing Family

No. 99349

This three bedroom, split-entry home can be expanded to grow with the family. The lower level of this home can be finished off as needed. The kitchen features a formal dining area and an eat-in area. The master suite has vaulted ceilings and a bay window provides views of the backyard. The living room overlooks the entry hall below.

Main & upper levels — 1,549 sq. ft.
Basement — 700 sq. ft.
Garage — 640 sq. ft.

Total living area — 1,549 sq. ft.

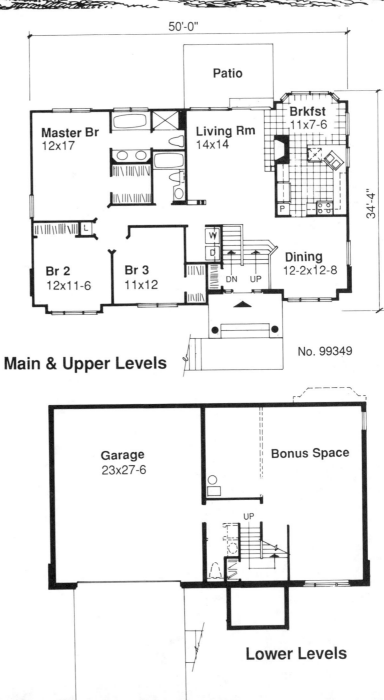

Main & Upper Levels

Lower Levels

Den Can Double As a Home Office

No. 90816

Traditional styling marks this elegant, four-bedroom home with lots of outdoor living space. Flooded with light from a picture window, the sunken living room lies just off the central foyer. At the rear of the home, the kitchen is flanked by the formal dining room and a breakfast nook. Sliding glass doors open to the sundeck. A single step leads down to the fireplaced family room. Window gables at the top of the gently curving staircase provide pleasing study nooks. The master suite features a luxurious whirlpool bath.

First floor — 1,252 sq. ft.
Second floor — 1,117 sq. ft.
Unfinished basement —
1,245 sq. ft.
Garage — 564 sq. ft.
Width — 71 ft.
Depth — 35 ft.(plus 8 ft. sun deck)

Total living area — 2,369 sq. ft.

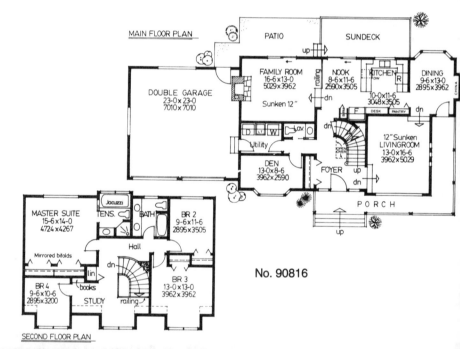

Country Home for Family Living

No. 10634

With a graceful porch sheltering three sides of this inviting home and a patio off the back, you can enjoy all your summer evenings outside. Walk out for a breath of fresh air after enjoying the formal dining room or the sunny breakfast nook. The adjoining kitchen and cozy family room are located across the central foyer from the spacious living room. Sharing the second floor with three bedrooms and two baths, the master suite features a hexagonal sitting room.

First floor — 1,182 sq. ft.
Second floor — 1,164 sq. ft.

Total living area — 2,346 sq. ft.

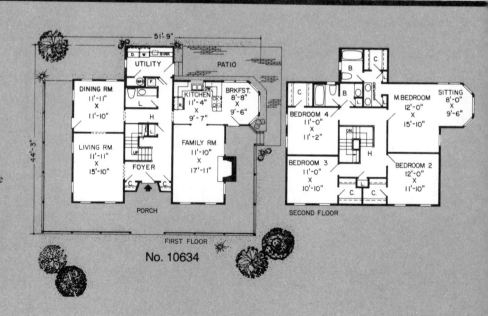

Spacious Columned Veranda

No. 91712

A spacious columned veranda, and a captain's walk above the door, all add to the Victorian charm of this home. Windows curve across the oval-shaped end of the living room as well as the master suite, located directly above it. Fireplaces, optional for both, are vented through a double chimney. The dining room, octagon in shape, also has a wall of windows. A wide U-shaped kitchen is located between the dining room and a nook/family room combination. In the center of the home are the pantry, utility room and half-bath making efficient use of space. An open staircase curves up the side of a wide foyer to the master suite and bedroom on the second level. The master suite has a generous step-in closet, and both the master bath and the bathroom feature double vanities, separate from the water closet.

First floor — 1,210 sq. ft.
Second floor — 919 sq. ft.

FIRST FLOOR PLAN

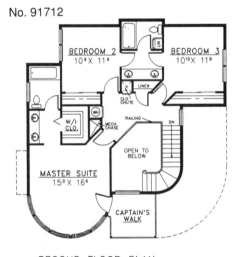

SECOND FLOOR PLAN

Width — 39'-0''
Depth — 44'-0''

Total living area — 2,129 sq. ft.

Lots of Living in Four-bedroom Starter

No. 10520

This traditional exterior, with its charming dormers, provides four bedrooms and lots of style even on a small lot. The very large master suite on the second floor includes the luxury of a jacuzzi. The other second floor bedroom also has a private bath and a walk-in closet. On the first floor are two more bedrooms which share a bath. The living room is reminiscent of the old-fashioned parlor. The dining area and U-shaped kitchen are located toward the back of the house overlooking the lawn and provide an ideal setting for family meals.

First floor — 960 sq. ft.
Second floor — 660 sq. ft.
Basement — 960 sq. ft.

Total living area — 1,620 sq. ft.

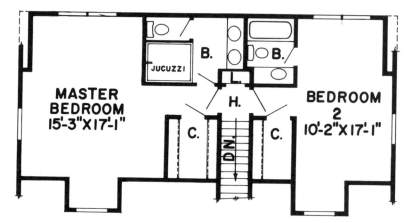

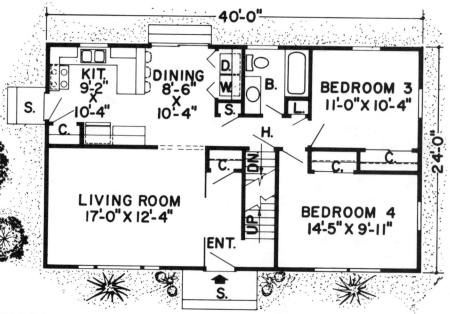

A Touch of Classic Elegance

No. 20079

There's no wasted space in this compact home that combines the best of classic design and modern convenience. If you're a traditionalist, you'll love the half-round windows, clapboard and brick facade, and cozy fireplace. But, from the moment you walk past the portico, you'll find exciting contemporary touches: soaring ceilings, a dramatic balcony, a U-shaped kitchen, and wide-open living areas. Laundry facilities are conveniently adjacent to downstairs bedrooms. You'll enjoy retreating upstairs to your very private master suite.

First floor — 1,200 sq. ft.
Second floor — 461 sq. ft.
Garage — 475 sq. ft.
Basement — 1,200 sq. ft.

Total living area — 1,661 sq. ft.

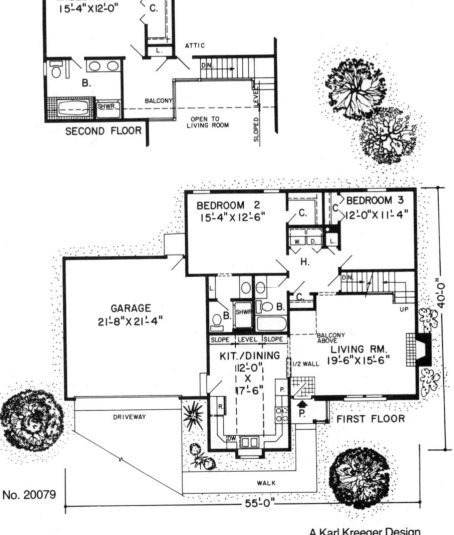

A Karl Kreeger Design

FmHA Approved

Just Starting Out

No. 92034

This 1,008 square foot ranch plan for 2 or more occupants is the perfect home for the family just starting out. The galley kitchen, with access to the attached garage, features laundry facilities and open dining area. The large living room allows plenty of room for entertaining. The single-car attached garage has plenty of room for routine vehicle maintenance and lawn mower storage.

Main living area — 1,008 sq. ft.
Garage — 2-Car

**Total living area — 1,008 sq. ft.
2 or More Occupants**

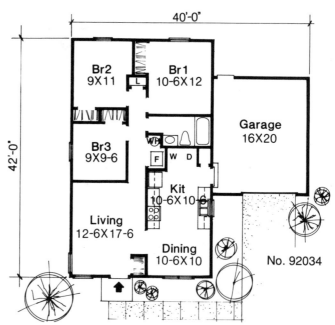

Single-Level Living

No. 99329

For the move-up or empty-nester buyer who is looking for lots of features, but wants them all on one floor, consider this 1,642 square foot home. The interior offers many surprises like a vaulted ceiling in the living room and a built-in plant shelf. A fireplace forms the focus of this room. The angled kitchen has a sunny breakfast room. The formal dining room has stately divider details. Two bedrooms and two full baths in the sleeping wing of the home include the master suite.

Main living area — 1,642 sq. ft.
Garage — 2-car

Total living area — 1,642 sq. ft.

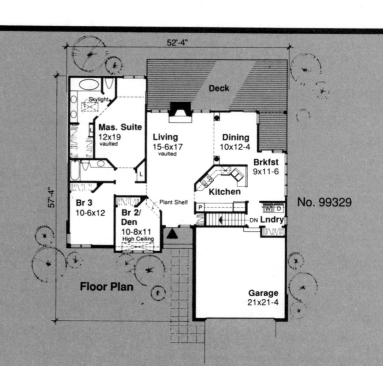

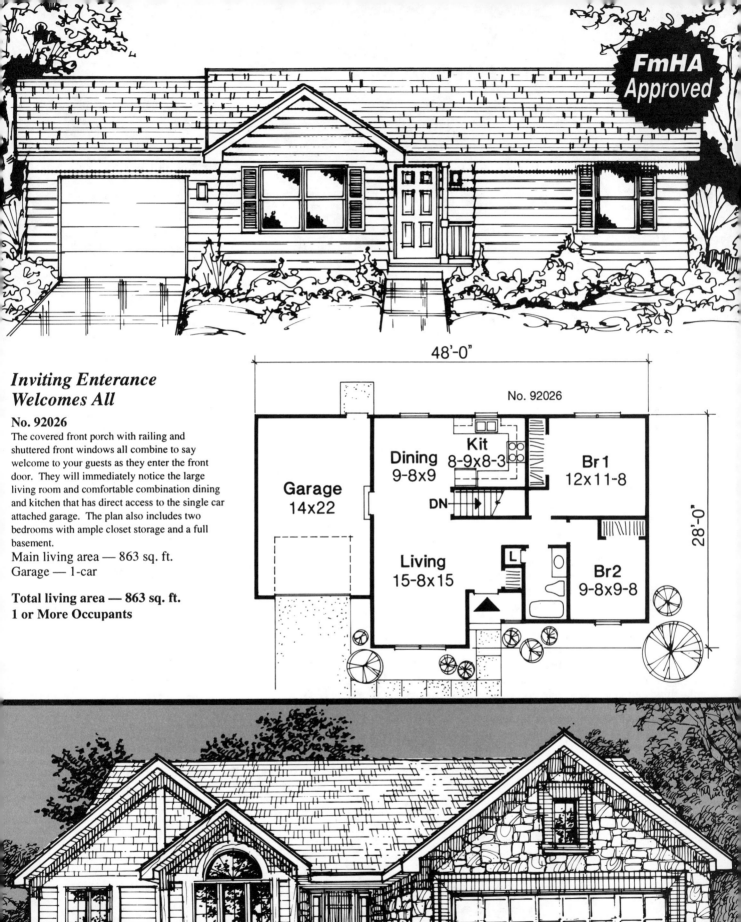

Inviting Enterance Welcomes All

No. 92026

The covered front porch with railing and shuttered front windows all combine to say welcome to your guests as they enter the front door. They will immediately notice the large living room and comfortable combination dining and kitchen that has direct access to the single car attached garage. The plan also includes two bedrooms with ample closet storage and a full basement.

Main living area — 863 sq. ft.
Garage — 1-car

Total living area — 863 sq. ft.
1 or More Occupants

Outdoor-Lovers' Delight
No. 10748

This one-level charmer packs a lot of convenience into a compact space. From the shelter of the front porch, the foyer leads three ways: right to the bedroom wing, left to the roomy kitchen and dining room, or straight ahead to the massive living room. You'll appreciate the quiet atmosphere in the sleeping wing, the elegant recessed ceilings and private bath in the master suite, and the laundry facilities that adjoin the bedrooms. You'll enjoy the convenience of a kitchen with a built-in pantry and adjacent dining room. And, you'll love the airy atmosphere in the sunny, fireplaced living room, which features a cooling fan, high ceilings, and double French doors to the huge, wrap-around porch.

Main living area — 1,540 sq. ft.
Porches — 530 sq. ft.

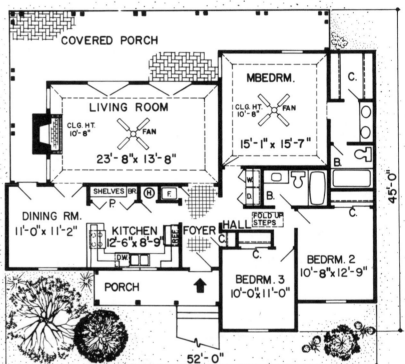

Total living area — 1,540 sq. ft.

No. 10748

Simple Lines Enhanced by Elegant Window Treatment

No. 34150

Consider this plan if you work at home and would enjoy a homey, well-lit office or den. The huge, arched window floods the front room with light. This house offers a lot of other practical details for the two-career family. Compact and efficient use of space means less to clean and organize. Yet the open plan keeps the home from feeling too small and cramped. Other features like plenty of closet space, step-saving laundry facilities, easily-cleaned kitchen, and a window wall in the living room make this a delightful plan.

Main living area — 1,492 sq. ft.
Garage — 462 sq. ft.
Basement — 1,486 sq. ft.

Total living area — 1,492 sq. ft.

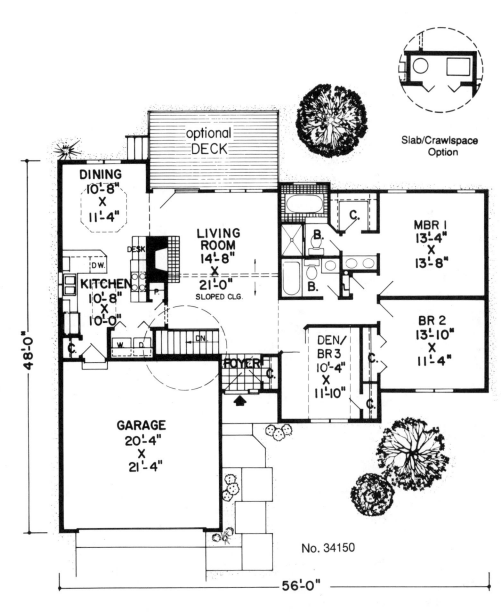

Fabulous Facade

No. 91604

The facade of this magnificent brick masterpiece, with its massive covered arch and towering window, provides an impressive introduction to entering guests. Show them into the cozy den off the foyer for quiet conversation, or the formal living and dining room arrangement for a festive affair. The gourmet kitchen with its convenient cooktop island will make entertaining easy. In the adjoining family room, generous windows combine with a crackling fire for warmth in any weather. Step up the stairs to find a full bath which serves the kids' rooms and the bonus room. The master suite is your special retreat, featuring a coved ceiling, sumptuous bath with garden tub, and room-sized walk-in closet.

First floor — 1,200 sq. ft.
Second floor — 1,020 sq. ft.
Bonus room — 246 sq. ft.
Garage — 2-car

Total living area — 2,466 sq. ft.

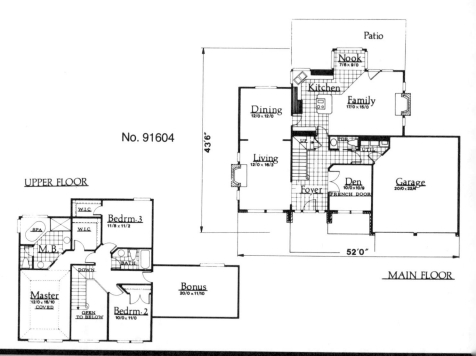

Family-Preferred Features in Tudor Design

No. 10568

Many family-preferred features are offered in this deluxe Tudor design. An energy efficient foyer leads into a Great room that has its own wood-burning fireplace. Off of the Great room lies the master bedroom, the only bedroom on the first level. The master bedroom has its own private wood deck, and the bath area has a two way shower and a his-and-her bathroom space with separate facilities. Also on the first level is an efficient kitchen with a large breakfast nook, and just off the kitchen is a utility room. The second level includes a cedar closet, a loft area that overlooks the Great room below, and two bedrooms that share a full bath.

First floor — 2,167 sq. ft.
Second floor — 755 sq. ft.
Basement — 2,224 sq. ft.
Garage — 1,020 sq. ft.

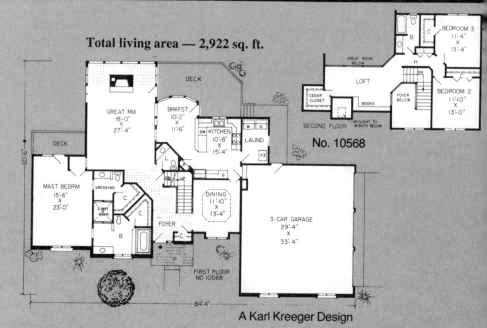

A Karl Kreeger Design

Gracious Exterior, Gracious Living

No. 99609

Comfortable and gracious living is the theme of this home. At the entrance foyer, the well-lit decorative stair creates a good first impression. The two-story living room terminating in a handsome heat-circulating fireplace and the rear glass wall intensifies that good feeling. Other features are the octagonal dining room, the kitchen, combination dinette and family room also with a fireplace and the den or bedroom which actually is an all-purpose room. A huge terrace extends along the entire rear. The second floor features a large bay window in the master bedroom with dressing room and large walk-in closet. The bathroom has a whirlpool tub and two basins. Walk-in closets are included in the other two bedrooms. Part of the bedroom hall dramatically overlooks the living room.

First floor — 1,142 sq. ft.
Second floor — 978 sq. ft.
Lndry/mudroom — 59 sq. ft.
Garage — 428 sq. ft.

Total living area — 2,120 sq. ft.

No. 99609

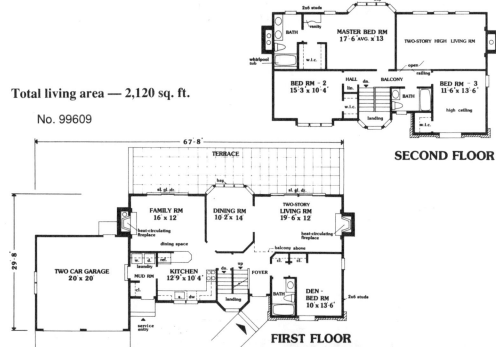

Simplicity in Design
No. 6687

Reminiscent of past years of open porches and large rooms, this design appeals to the first time home owner. Simplicity can best describe this small ranch house with its kitchen and utility room appropriately positioned for economy of space. A formal dining area lists off from the kitchen, while an open living room with its wood-burning fireplace adds comfort and relaxation. A dressing table in the bath area is another added luxury in this design. The bedrooms are highlighted by four windows making the rooms brighter with natural lighting. Large closets are featured in the bedrooms.

Main floor — 1,380 sq. ft.
Porches — 240 sq. ft.

Total living area — 1,380 sq. ft.

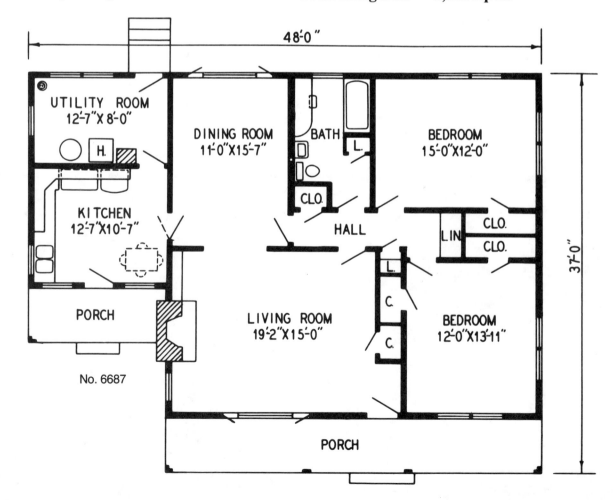

Focus on Family Activities

No. 90124

The whole family will enjoy the arrangement of this traditionally styled three-bedroom home. Family and guests alike will be drawn to the cozy family room that opens onto the patio. The warm fireplace and beamed ceiling spread their charm to the adjacent kitchen, which easily serves the counter area and the formal dining room. The mudroom entrance is made even more practical by combining it with laundry facilities. A 3/4 bath completes the first floor. Each of the 3 roomy bedrooms on the second floor has ample closet space with the master suite enjoying a large walk-in closet. Please specify basement or crawl space foundation when ordering.

First floor — 1,080 sq. ft.
Second floor — 868 sq. ft.

Total living area — 1,948 sq. ft.

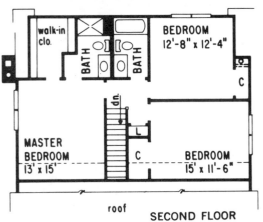

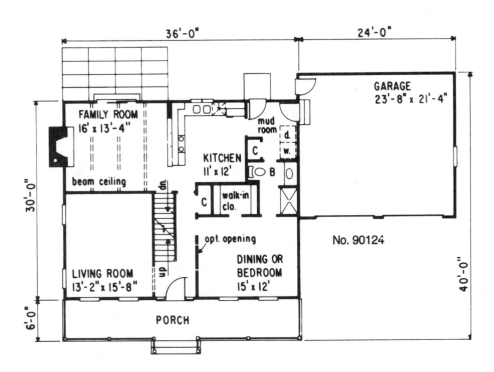

A Lifetime Home

No. 91662

This beautiful, very popular plan has been re-designed to allow accessibility for a lifetime of use. It has built-in features that make modification possible to accommodate the permanently disabled, the elderly or even temporary disabled due to sports injuries, surgery, etc... Wider hallways and doors, specially designed baths and kitchen, and low profile thresholds are among some of the features you will find. No materials list available for this plan.

Main floor — 2,167 sq. ft.
Lower floor — 1,154 sq. ft.

Total living area —3,321 sq. ft.

No materials list available

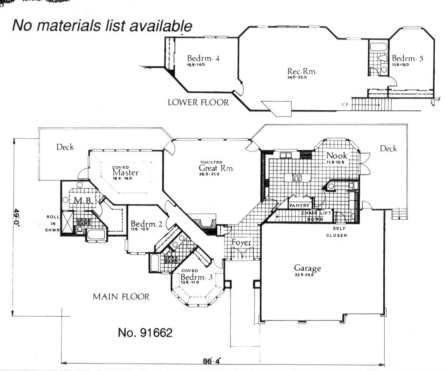

Stone Facade Accents Five-Bedroom Home

No. 10530

Double-door entry leads to other first floor features including a hearth room with wood stove, window seat and built-in desk; master bedroom with fireplace, five-piece bath and private greenhouse entrance; multi-windowed Great room with fireplace and deck access. Upstairs are four bedrooms, two baths, a study and a cedar closet.

First floor — 2,344 sq. ft.
Second floor — 1,382 sq. ft.
Basement — 2,344 sq. ft.
Garage — 781 sq. ft.
Shop — 286 sq. ft.

Total living area — 3,726 sq. ft.

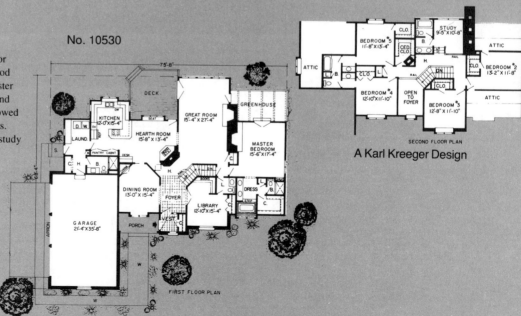

A Karl Kreeger Design

Expandable French Provincial Features Three to Five Bedrooms

No. 90402

This lovely home features a master suite with a deluxe compartmentalized bath which includes a vaulted ceiling with skylights, garden tub, shower, linen closet and a separate dressing room with a double vanity and a large walk-in closet. Two additional bedrooms with ample closet space share a second compartmentalized bath. Living and dining rooms are located to the side of the formal foyer. A family room with a formal fireplace and double doors on to a screened-in back porch and a U-shaped kitchen with an island counter open to the breakfast bay to allow more casual living. Open rail stairs in the family room provide access to the second floor. The second floor can be either unfinished or finished with one or two bedrooms and a large bath. Please specify a basement, crawl space or slab foundation when ordering.

First floor — 2,400 sq. ft.
Second floor — 751 sq. ft.

Total living area — 3,151 sq. ft.

No. 90402

A Country Classic
No. 99334

The traditional country estate home is revived in this 2,644 square foot design. Outside, repeated front projecting gables, covered front entry, divided windows and three-car garage all give the house an estate look. The home's entry has an exciting view of the formal living and dining rooms separated by columns. The rear family room has a vaulted-ceiling, open rail stairs and fireplace. The island kitchen has easy access to the breakfast area and laundry/mud room. The first floor master suite features a double door entry, vaulted ceiling with plant shelf, and large walk-in closet. The spacious master bath has an oval tub under glass, separate shower, compartmental toilet and angled double vanity.

Main floor — 1,933 sq. ft.
Upper floor — 711 sq. ft.
Garage — 3-car

Total living area — 2,644 sq. ft.

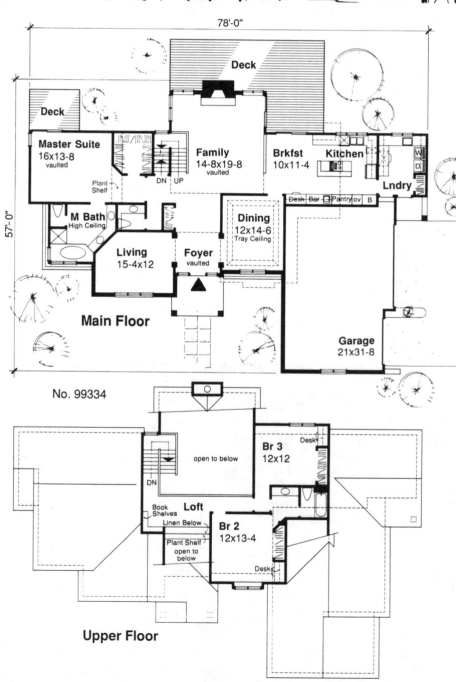

Compact Traditional for Easy Living

No. 34976

This Ranch features a handsome facade accentuated by a gabled bay window and a tidy porch. The living and dining rooms off the foyer flow together opposite the centrally-located family room and kitchen. The breakfast nook and family room share a view of the backyard through the optional attached screened porch. The two front bedrooms share a full bath and the master suite includes a walk-in closet and a full bath. The laundry room, located for convenience, serves as a sound buffer for the bedroom wing. The optional attached garage has a handy inside entry near the kitchen.

Main living area — 1,786 sq. ft.
Basement — 1,775 sq. ft.
Garage — 426 sq. ft.
Optional screened porch — 223 sq. ft.

Total living area — 1,786 sq. ft.

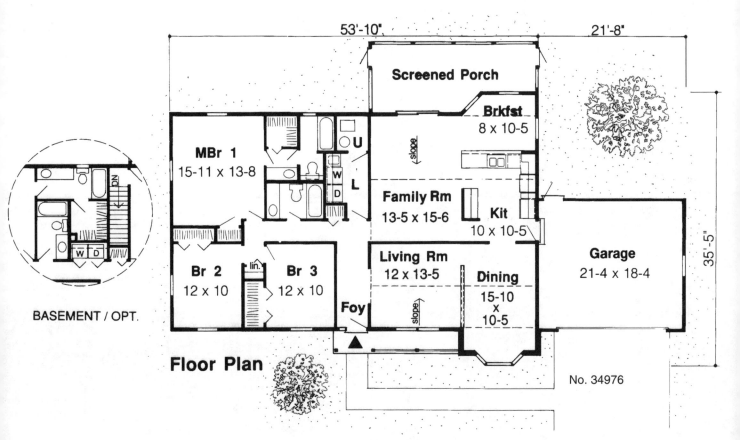

A Traditional Farmhouse

No. 99626

Charming and friendly, this farmhouse Colonial captures the early American style with its traditional front porch, shuttered double hung windows, and wood siding. Conductive to outdoor living are the porch in the rear and large terrace. Once inside, the family room and dinette flow together in a well-defined and compatible design. The center hall arrangement features a decorative circular stairway to the second floor. Here, the master suite is situated with a fully-equipped bathroom including shower stall, two basins, and a whirlpool tub. A huge walk-in closet allows for an abundance of storage. Although the room sizes are spacious, the simplicity of construction and design make this home affordable.

First floor — 1,183 sq. ft.
Second floor — 1,103 sq. ft.
Basement — 1,116 sq. ft.
Garage — 467 sq. ft.

Total living area — 2,286 sq. ft.

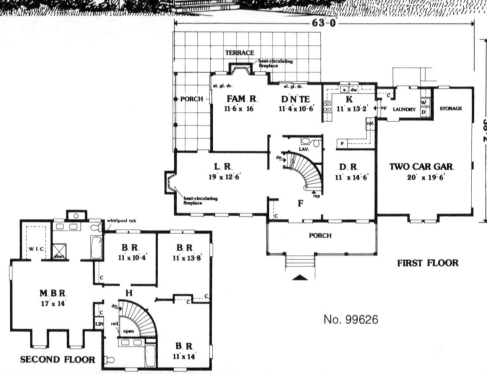

Formal Entry, Luxury Master Suite, Plus Room to Expand

No. 34825

In addition to the three well-designed bedrooms, the second floor of this traditional design features a large unfinished area which could be a study, hobby center, or even a fully-equipped exercise room. The luxury master suite has two walk-in closets in the dressing area plus a conveniently arranged five-piece bath which features a circular window above the tiled tub enclosure. The first floor is composed of formal dining and living rooms on either side of the tiled foyer with the family areas organized along the back overlooking the patio. The cozy family room has a fireplace, built-in bookcase and opens onto the patio. The kitchen features a bump-out window over the sink and shares a snack bar with the bright and cheery breakfast nook.

First floor — 1,212 sq. ft.
Second floor — 1,030 sq. ft.
Basement — 1,212 sq. ft.
Garage — 521 sq. ft.

Total living area — 2,242 sq. ft.

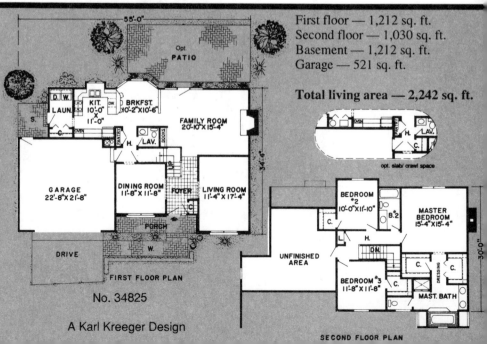

A Karl Kreeger Design

Detailed Victorian Design

No. 99624

Comfortable living is expressed in this 4 bedroom plus studio Victorian house. The delicate details, wood siding, curved shingles, bays, dormers and steep roof are characteristic of this style. Featured are the farmhouse front porch, the curved ornamental stair in the spacious foyer, heat-circulating fireplace in the living room, large glass areas in the family room and dinette and bay windows in the kitchen and dining room. In addition, the second floor features two luxurious bathrooms each having 2 basins — the master bath also has a stall shower. The master bedroom is equipped with a walk-in closet and two additional closets. The house shows a full basement but can be built as a slab on grade if desired.

First floor — 2,397 sq. ft.
Studio — 312 sq. ft.
Garage — 434 sq. ft.

Total living area — 2,709 sq. ft

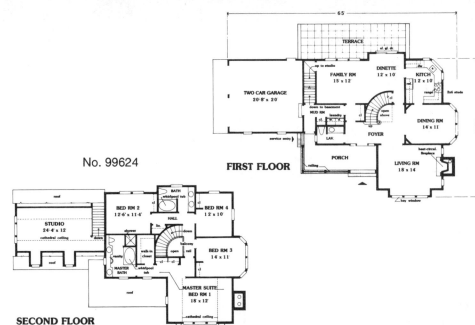

Classic Colonial Style With Modern Floor Plan

No. 90449

This Colonial two-story home has the exterior features of long ago, but the interior is designed for today's living. The entry foyer is flanked on either side by the formal living and dining rooms. The large family room has a fireplace with book-shelves, and French doors leading to an outdoor deck. The spacious kitchen is open to the breakfast room, which has a bay window. Upstairs, the master suite is large enough for most furniture, and the master bath has a corner garden tub and separate shower. The walk-in closet has plenty of hanging space. Two other bedrooms share another full bath. The laundry room is also located on the second floor, which should please the homemaker. The optional bonus room can be finished for an extra bedroom, playroom or office. This plan is available with either a basement or crawl space foundation. Please specify when ordering.

First floor — 1,138 sq. ft.
Second floor — 1,124 sq. ft.
Optional bonus — 284 sq. ft.
Basement — 1,124 sq. ft.
Garage — 484 sq. ft.

Total living area — 2,262 sq. ft.

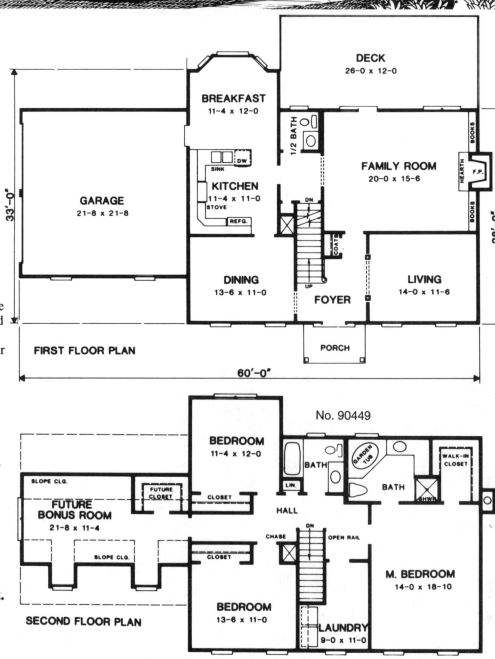

102

From Times Gone By

No. 24301

Reminiscent of a simpler time, yet up-to-date on the conveniences we have come to depend on. The front porch is a warm welcome at the end of the day. Come inside to the large living room, great for entertaining. Or relax in your family room which opens to your deck. Upstairs the master bedroom has its own bath and ample closet space. The secondary bedrooms, of which there are three, share the hall bath and each have lots of closet space. Family living at its best!

Main level — 987 sq. ft.
Upper level — 970 sq. ft.
Basement — 985 sq. ft.

Total living area — 1,957 sq. ft.

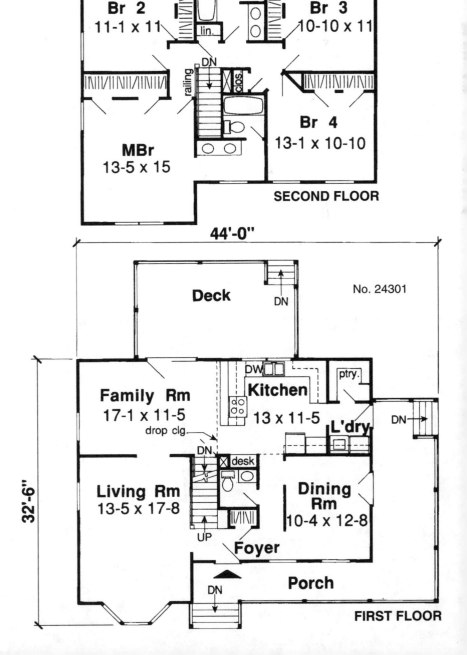

Southern Colonial Design

No. 10577

This southern colonial design of grand styling offers many oppulent features for homeowners. Stately columns stand out from its brick exterior that also has a dash of wood veneer siding. Double doors lead to a spacious foyer which has closet space close by. Past the foyer is a half bath. To the right of the foyer is the living room and a family room. The family room has a wood-burning fireplace. To the left of the foyer is the dining room and the breakfast room. The kitchen is open to the breakfast room and to the left of the kitchen is the laundry room and the garage. The second level has four bedrooms and two full baths. Other exciting features of this design include the use of French doors that lead out to a brick patio from both the breakfast and the dining rooms.

First floor — 1,490 sq. ft.
Second floor — 1,183 sq. ft.
Basement — 1,376 sq. ft.
Garage — 537 sq. ft.

Total living area — 2,673 sq. ft.

Greek Revival

No. 99610

The large front entrance porch with its pediment and columns, although classical in style, presents a farmhouse quality. The 11'-0" ceiling height for the foyer and 25 foot long living room, the focal point of which is a stunning, brick-faced, heat-circulating fireplace flanked by cabinetry and shelves, give a spacious feeling throughout. The formal dining room with a bayed window, connects to the living room and kitchen and overlooks a large rear terrace. The private bedroom wing, separately zoned from the main active living spaces, contains three bedrooms and two baths. One bath with two basins and a whirlpool tub serves the master bedroom while the other is shared by the other two bedrooms. The master bath has sliding glass doors which connect to a private terrace.

Main living area — 1,460 sq. ft.
Lndry/mudroom — 68 sq. ft.
Garage & Storage — 494 sq. ft.
Basement — 1,367 sq. ft.

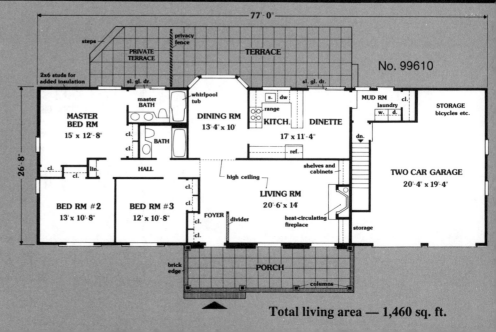

Total living area — 1,460 sq. ft.

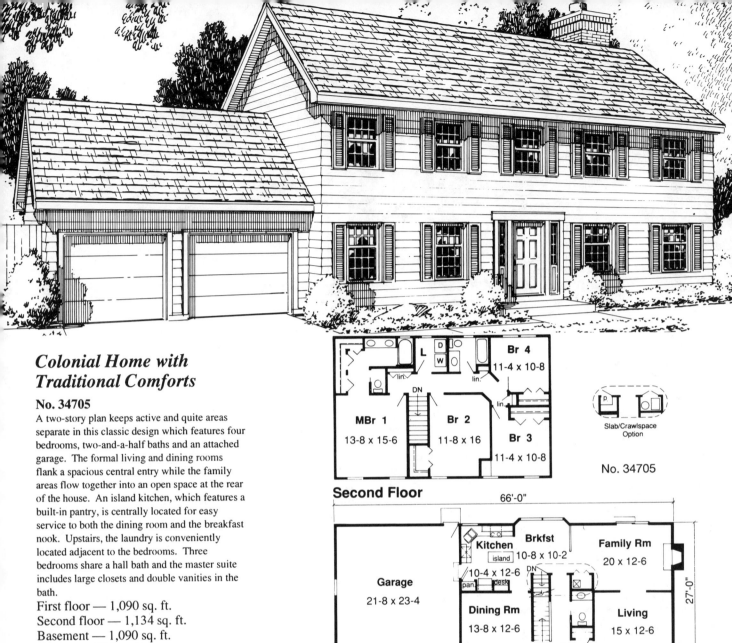

Colonial Home with Traditional Comforts

No. 34705

A two-story plan keeps active and quite areas separate in this classic design which features four bedrooms, two-and-a-half baths and an attached garage. The formal living and dining rooms flank a spacious central entry while the family areas flow together into an open space at the rear of the house. An island kitchen, which features a built-in pantry, is centrally located for easy service to both the dining room and the breakfast nook. Upstairs, the laundry is conveniently located adjacent to the bedrooms. Three bedrooms share a hall bath and the master suite includes large closets and double vanities in the bath.

First floor — 1,090 sq. ft.
Second floor — 1,134 sq. ft.
Basement — 1,090 sq. ft.
Garage — 576 sq. ft.

Total living area — 2,224 sq. ft.

Built-In Beauty

No. 90942

The brick and stucco exterior of this beautiful home encloses a spacious plan designed for convenience. A huge, sunken living room with vaulted ceilings flows into the formal dining room overlooking the backyard. Eat here, or in the nook on the other side of the adjoining kitchen. An open railing and a single stair separate the nook and the fireplaced family room, each featuring sliding glass doors to the patio. Notice the built-ins throughout the house that help keep clutter down, and the handy bath tucked behind the garage. Three bedrooms up the open staircase include the expansive master suite with private dressing room, walk-in closet, and double-vanitied bath with step-in shower.

First floor — 1,175 sq. ft.
Second floor — 776 sq. ft.
Basement — 1,165 sq. ft.
Garage — 410 sq. ft.
Width — 44' - 0"
Depth — 46' - 6"

Total living area — 1,951 sq. ft.

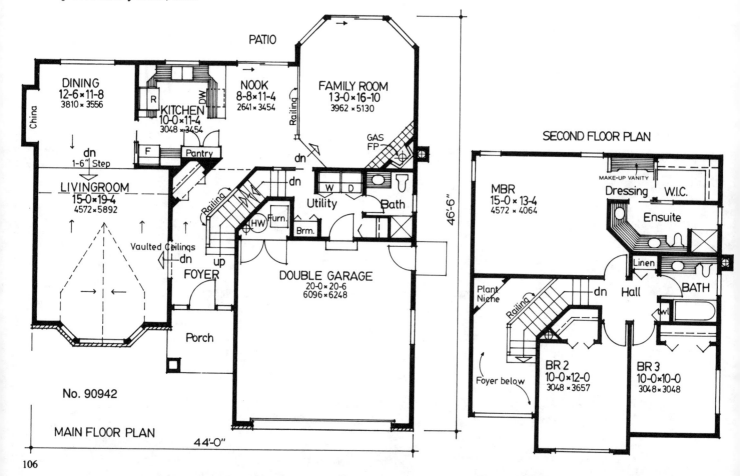

Dormer Enhanced Dining Room

No. 91353

This two-story traditional home boasts a total of 1,633 sq. ft. The vaulted entry leads to the living room accented with a bay window, or to the vaulted dining room with built-in china cabinets. The kitchen, with an abundance of cabinets, and the sunny breakfast bay merge into a useful open space. Nearby is a half-bath and a laundry room that leads to a double-car garage. The family room is kept cozy by a woodstove. The master bedroom suite has a private bath and naturally lighted closet, plus an additional 5 ft. standard closet.

Main floor — 950 sq. ft.
Upper floor — 683 sq. ft.
Garage — 2-car

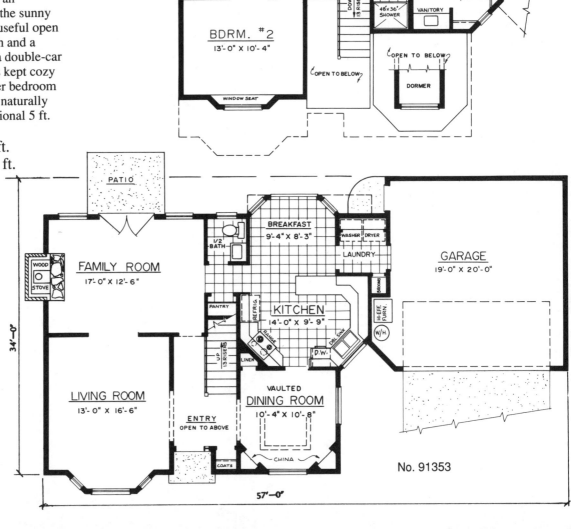

Total living area — 1,633 sq. ft.

No. 91353

Flexible, Award-Winning Design

No. 19938

This two-story home is ideal for those on a budget looking for an adaptable design. The primary living areas on the lower floor complete the basic one-bedroom plan, leaving the upper level, breezeway and garage for completion later, if necessary. The two rooms on the upper level could be used as bedrooms, a hobby room, private office, or almost anything you choose. The family/dining/living areas are open to the multi-purpose room above and only partially divided from one another, creating a more spacious and formal atmosphere. You're sure to find that this plan offers a lot for a little.

First floor — 1,090 sq. ft.
Second floor — 580 sq. ft.
Garage — 484 sq. ft.

Total living area — 1,670 sq. ft.

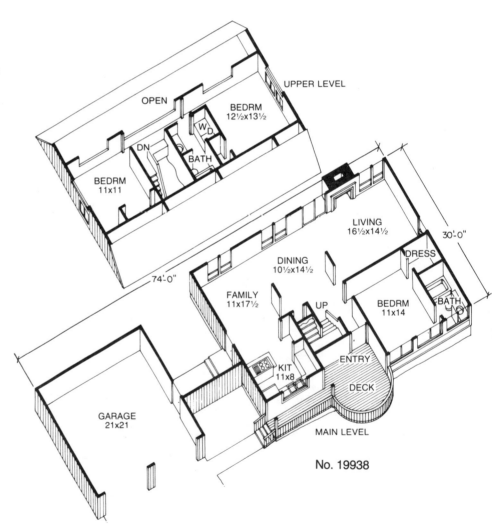

108

Country Colonial

No. 99210

Revel in the sheer spaciousness of this elegant, four-bedroom home, with its dramatic cathedral entry and balcony overlook. The two family rooms — one up, one down — feature a two-story, divided window wall and are perfect for entertaining, recreation, and family togetherness. Imagine those quiet summer evenings relaxing on either of the two covered porches. You'll love cooking in this well-planned kitchen that opens onto a sunny, "greenhouse" breakfast room. There's plenty of convenience here: abundant storage, extra-large laundry and mudroom, and three-and-a-half baths, including separate his-n-her dressing/bath suites.

First floor — 2,116 sq. ft.
Second floor — 1,848 sq. ft.
Garage — 667 sq. ft.

Total living area — 3,964 sq. ft.

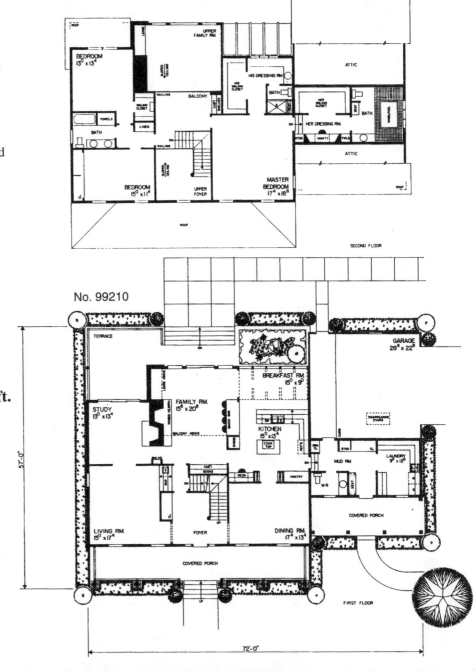

Ranch Provides Great Floor Plan

No. 34055

This great ranch features a front porch to sit and admire your view. A large living room and dining room flow together into one open space perfect for entertaining. The laundry room, which doubles as a mudroom, is off the kitchen and a back door entrance gives easy access to the outside. A master suite includes a private bathroom and the three additional bedrooms share a bathroom. A double-car garage is included in this plan.

Main living area — 1,527 sq. ft.
Basement — 1,344 sq. ft.
Garage — 425 sq. ft.

Total living area — 1,527 sq. ft.

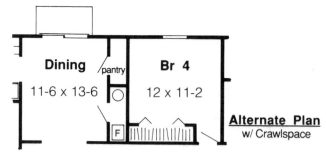

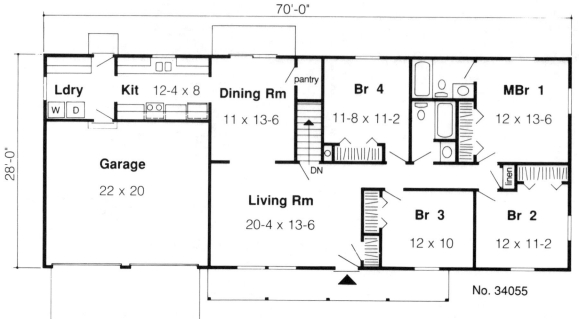

Impressive Entry Crowned by Clerestory Window

No. 34681

The split foyer entry of this charmer has a half-flight of stairs that leads down to a family room, a utility room, a powder room, a study, and a two-car garage. Step up to a large living room, an adjoining dining room and kitchen. A hall bath serves the two front bedrooms tucked down the hall while the rear master suite features a private bath.

Upper floor — 1,331 sq. ft.
Lower floor — 663 sq. ft.
Garage — 584 sq. ft.

Total living area — 1,994 sq. ft.

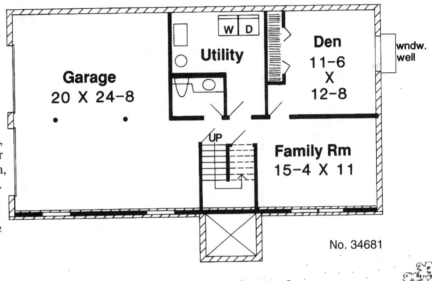

Lower Level

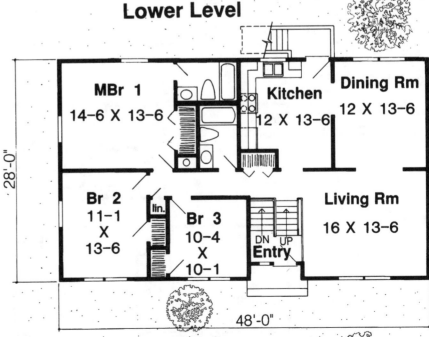

Floor Plan

Charming and Cozy Rooms

No. 90126

Here is a home that balances both individual and family needs. The traditional design encloses ample space for a large family, while preserving areas for comfort and quiet. The large family room, with cozy fireplace and sliding doors to the patio, is far away from the living room to simplify entertaining. Complementing the formal dining room is an eat-in nook. The efficiently organized kitchen serves either area well. Upstairs, the master bedroom has a large walk-in closet. Two other bedrooms are nearby for night-time security. This plan is available with a basement or crawl space foundation. Please specify when ordering.

First floor — 1,260 sq. ft.
Second floor — 952 sq. ft.

Total living area — 2,212 sq. ft.

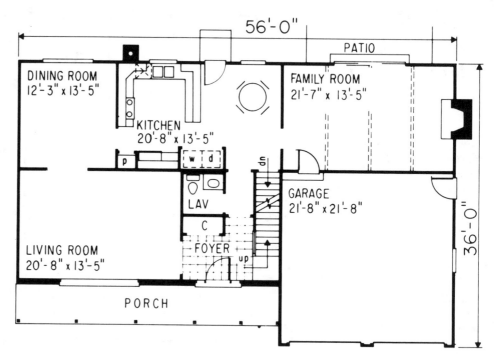

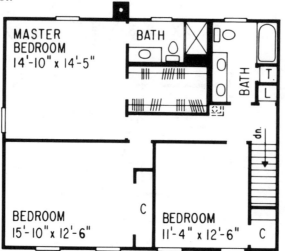

SECOND FLOOR

No. 90126

112

Expand with Ease

No. 99365

This three bedroom, split-entry home can be expanded to grow with the family. The kitchen features a formal dining area. The vaulted master suite with its many windows provide a sunny hideaway. The living room overlooks the entry below, adding eye appeal while you entertain. The lower level can be finished off as a family room as your family grows.

Main living area — 1,203 sq. ft.
Garage — 2-car

Total living area — 1,203 sq. ft.

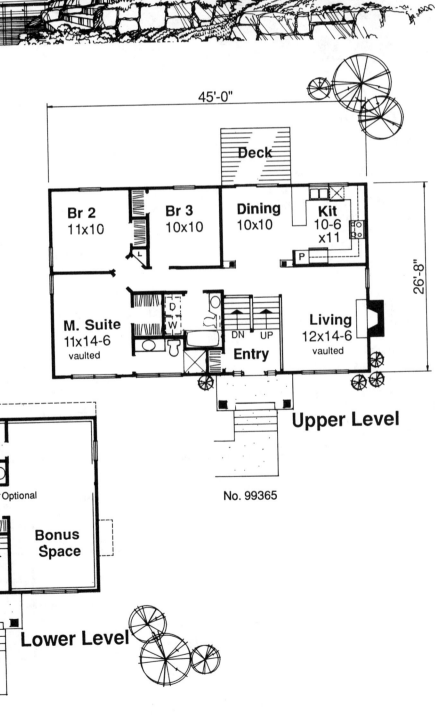

Classic and Comfortable
No. 90435

A central staircase dominates the spacious foyer of this efficient Tudor home. The convenient, L-shaped arrangement of kitchen, formal, and informal dining rooms means meal service will be a breeze. And, the elegance of a massive fireplace, French doors, and an adjoining rear deck make the Great room a special spot. With three bedrooms and two full baths, there's room for the whole family upstairs. Use the bayed study off the master suite as a nursery, or a quiet getaway for those rare moments when you have time to relax. This plan can be built with a basement, slab or crawl space foundation. Please specify when ordering.

First floor — 1,032 sq. ft.
Second floor — 1,050 sq. ft.
Garage — 2-car

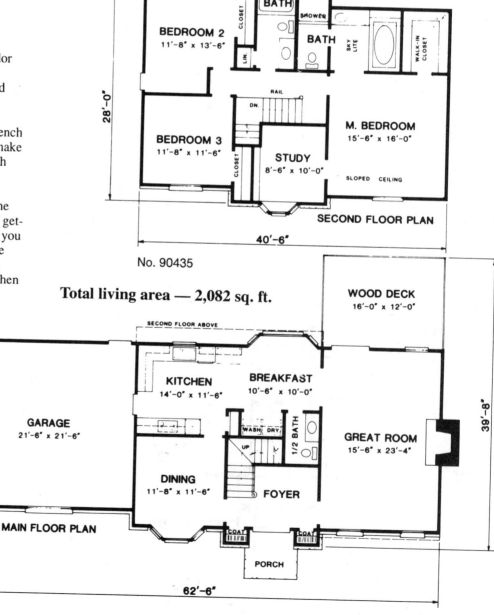

No. 90435
Total living area — 2,082 sq. ft.

Stately Manor

No. 90966

Here is a stately looking home that appears much larger than it really is. The grand entrance porch leads into a very spacious foyer with an open staircase and lots of angles. Note the beautiful kitchen with a full-bayed wall that includes the roomy breakfast nook. Meal preparation will be a delightful experience. The family room enjoys a fireplace and wetbar for cozy entertaining. The master suite, a retreat with its 5-piece private bath, shares the second floor with two other bedrooms and a hall bath.

First floor — 1,359 sq. ft.
Second floor — 1,038 sq. ft.
Basement — 1,334 sq. ft.
Garage — 420 sq. ft.
Width — 52'-0"
Depth — 43'-0"

Total living area —
  2,397 sq. ft.

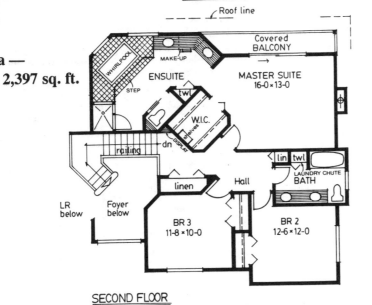

Efficient Yet Affordable
No. 34018

This two-story family home is great if you like to entertain. The living and dining rooms create one open space perfect for any party. The family areas offer lots of space and convenience with the kitchen just over the counter from both the sunny breakfast room and the fireplaced family room. Up the L-shaped stairs from the foyer are three bedrooms, laundry facilities and two full baths. The master suite boasts his-and-her closets and its own bath.

First floor — 980 sq. ft.
Second floor — 728 sq. ft.
Basement — 972 sq. ft.
Garage — 452 sq. ft.

Total living area — 1,708 sq. ft.

Slab/Crawlspace Option

No. 34018

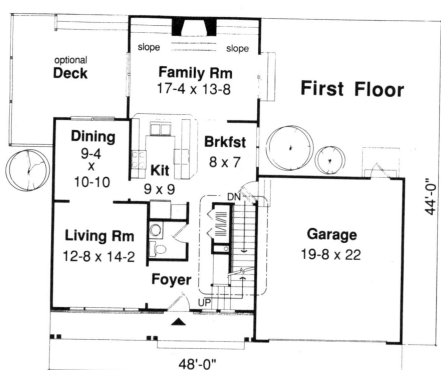

First Floor

Second Floor

Options Abound

No. 20061

This striking exterior features vertical siding, shake shingles, and stone, to off set a large picture window. Inside, the kitchen has a built-in pantry, refrigerator, dishwasher and range, breakfast bar, an open-beamed ceiling with a skylight, plus a breakfast area with lots of windows. A formal dining room complements the living room, which has two open beams running through a sloped-ceiling and a wood-burning fireplace. There is a laundry closet, and the foyer area also has a closet. Three bedrooms share a full bath. The master bedroom has an open-beamed, sloped-ceiling with a spacious bath area and a walk-in closet.

Main living area — 1,674 sq. ft.
Basement — 1,656 sq. ft.
Garage — 472 sq. ft.

Total living area — 1,674 sq. ft.

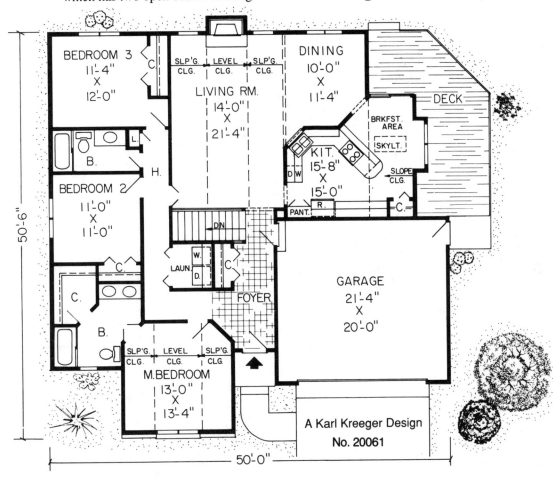

Gardener's Dream House

No. 20086

Start planning the landscaping. The shape of this delightful one-level home offers unlimited opportunities for a charming entry garden. And, with extra-large windows and a massive deck, you can enjoy every part of your yard in any season. This convenient plan unites living and dining rooms at the rear of the house. For family meals, the island kitchen features a cozy nook with easy access to the deck. Bedrooms, isolated in their own wing for maximum quiet, include a spacious master suite with skylit bath.

Basement — 1,628 sq. ft.
Garage — 434 sq. ft.

Total living area — 1,628 sq. ft.

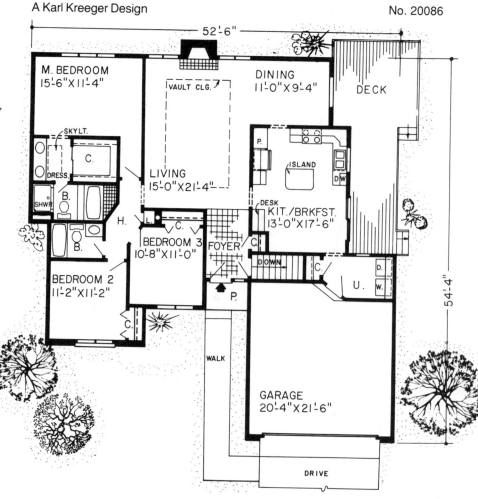

Huge Windows Create Cheerful Atmosphere

No. 91040

Are you looking for a family home that combines a contemporary open plan with a quiet bedroom wing? Here's a one-level gem that fills the bill. The three bedrooms, tucked away from active areas, include a spacious master suite with a private bath and enormous closet. You'll love the easy-care openness of the fireplaced living room, dining nook and kitchen. And, you can expand your outdoor living space through the sliding glass doors to the back...build a patio, porch, or deck to suit your yard. This plan is available with a crawl space foundation only.

Main living area — 1,206 sq. ft.
Garage — 2-car

Total living area — 1,206 sq. ft.

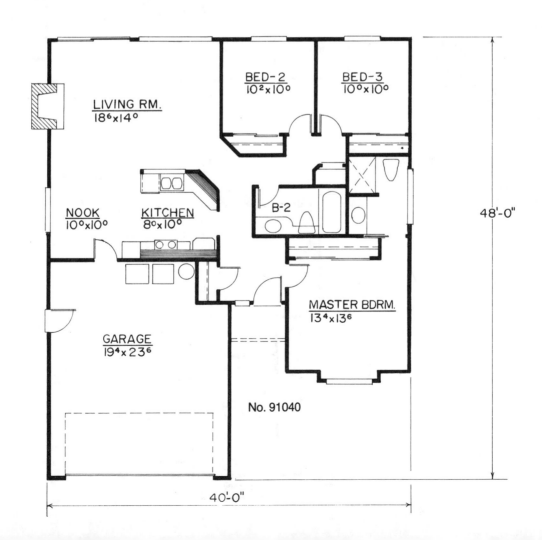

Impressive Use of Space

No. 90131

The Great room is the focal point of this uniquely organized plan; its sloped ceiling rises two stories to the cozy second-floor balcony. Also on the second floor is the master bedroom with its own balcony, double closets and roomy bath. The two first-floor bedrooms are separated from the living areas by the stairway, a large bath and extra closets. The L-shaped kitchen is conveniently located between the dining area and the garage entrance. Additional kitchen features are the built-in grill and the sliding door to the patio. The laundry room is placed so that it can also serve as a mudroom just inside the garage door. Specify basement or slab/crawl space foundation when ordering.

First floor — 1,320 sq. ft.
Second floor — 444 sq. ft.

Total living area — 1,764 sq. ft.

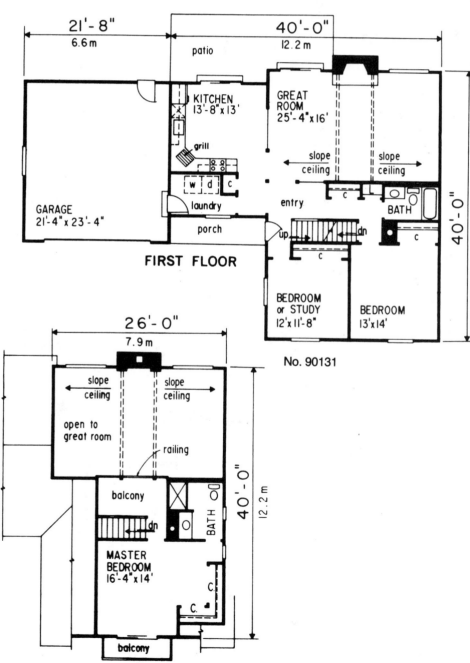

Traditional Styling

No. 90120

The lower level of this traditional home makes a great place for the family to work or play together. Behind the ample family room is a specially designed area that's just perfect for hobbies, crafts, sewing or whatever other activities your family might enjoy. In addition to the bath located on this level, there is space for two bedrooms or other work areas that you may wish to add in the future. The main level includes three bedrooms separated by a hall from the living, dining and kitchen areas.

Main level — 1,164 sq. ft.
Lower level — 1,108 sq. ft.

Total living area — 2,272 sq. ft.

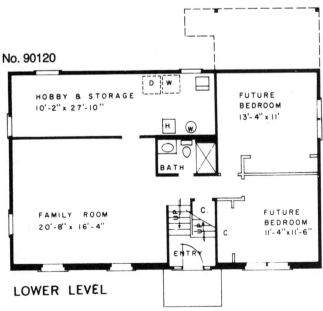

Graceful Curves for a Gracious Home
No. 10694

Does your family love the water? Treat them to this traditional brick four-bedroom beauty built around a circular in-ground pool. Family and breakfast rooms, living room, covered deck upstairs, and even the private master bedroom suite all overlook the expansive patio area. For formal entertaining away from the action, retreat to the formal dining room, just steps away from the kitchen.

First floor — 2,804 sq. ft.
Second floor — 848 sq. ft.
Garage — 673 sq. ft.

Total living area — 3,652 sq. ft.

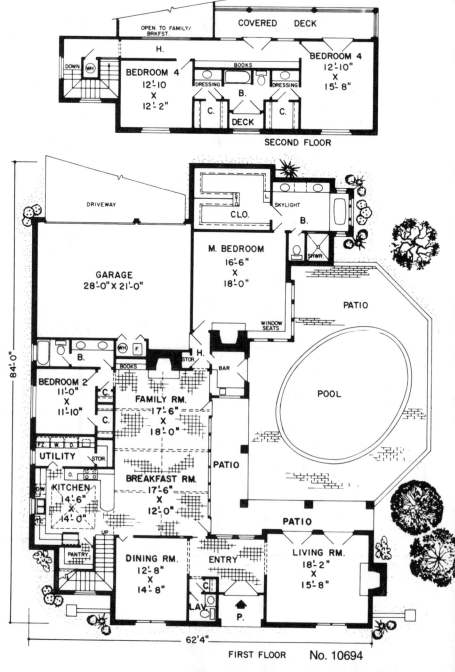

New England Tradition

No. 90608

This Salt Box classic appeals to almost everyone. It copies the best from the Colonial residential tradition and adds modern conveniences and efficiencies. A spacious foyer channels traffic to all parts of the house. The large, U-shaped kitchen serves the dinette, dining room, and patio. The ground floor bedroom can be easily adapted as a den; note the two entrances to the bath. Three bedrooms on the second floor have plenty of closet space. The master bedroom has a walk-in closet and well-equipped bath.

First floor — 1,195 sq. ft.
Second floor — 840 sq. ft.
Garage — 2-car

Total living area — 2,035 sq. ft.

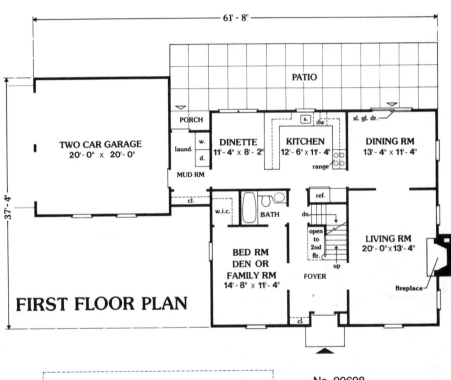

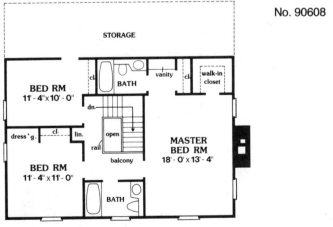

Porch Recalls a Romantic Era

No. 20098

Arched windows and a two-story bay lend an air of elegance to this exceptional four-bedroom beauty. Interior spaces are characterized by distinctive ceiling treatments, sloping ceilings pierced by skylights, and efficient room placements. Notice how easily the kitchen serves the hexagonal breakfast room, the formal dining room, and the adjoining deck. Even the fireplaced living room is only steps away. And, when the alarm rings early in the morning, you'll be grateful for the master suite's proximity to the coffee pot. The staircase off the foyer leads to three more bedrooms and a full, skylit bath with double vanities. Be sure to notice the wonderful angles and generous closet space in each room.

First floor — 1,843 sq. ft.
Second floor — 1,039 sq. ft.
Basement — 1,843 sq. ft.
Garage — 484 sq. ft.

Total living area — 2,882 sq. ft.

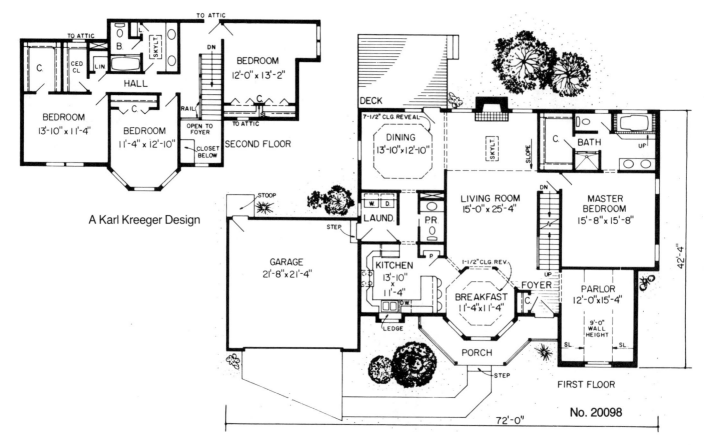

A Karl Kreeger Design

Elegant Master Suite Crowns Victorian

No. 20351

Gingerbread trim, round-top windows, and a two-story bay window bring a Victorian flavor to this modern plan. A fireplace adds a cozy charm to the angular living room just off the foyer. Walk past the stairs and the handy powder room to the rear of the house. Flanked by the formal dining and family rooms, the convenient kitchen lets the cook enjoy family activities and prepare dinner, too! You'll appreciate the outdoor living space the rear deck adds. But, when there's a chill in the air, you can light a fire and enjoy the view from the window seat in the family room. Three upstairs bedrooms include the bayed master suite, which features loads of closet space, a raised whirlpool tub, and a step-in shower for busy mornings.

First floor — 1,304 sq. ft.
Second floor — 1,009 sq. ft.
Basement — 1,304 sq. ft.
Garage — 688 sq. ft.

Total living area — 2,313 sq. ft.

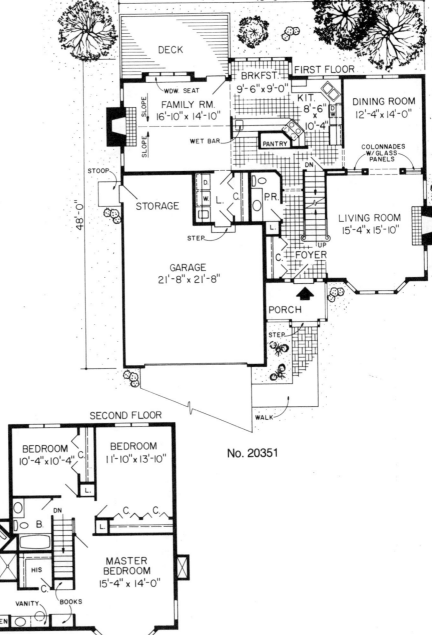

No. 20351

Basement Plan has Drive-Under Garage

No. 90401

This rustic design includes a two-car garage as part of its full basement. All or part of the basement can be used to supplement the main living area. The master suite features a large walk-in closet and a double vanity. The second level contains two bedrooms, two walk-in closets and a full bath. A front porch, multi-paned windows, shutters and horizontal wood siding combine for a rustic exterior. Please specify a basement or crawl space foundation when ordering.

First floor — 1,100 sq. ft.
Second floor — 660 sq. ft.

Total living area — 1,760 sq. ft.

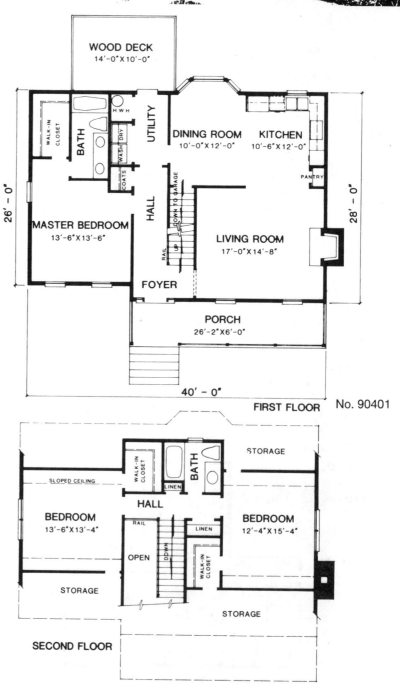

Impressive Entry Crowned by Clerestory Window

No. 34679

The split-foyer entry of this charmer has a half-flight of stairs that leads down to a family room, a utility room, a powder room, a study, and a two-car garage. Step up to a large living room, an adjoining dining room and kitchen. A hall bath serves the two front bedrooms tucked down the hall while the rear master suite features a private bath.

Upper floor — 1,331 sq. ft.
Lower floor — 663 sq. ft.
Garage — 584 sq. ft.

Total living area — 1,994 sq. ft.

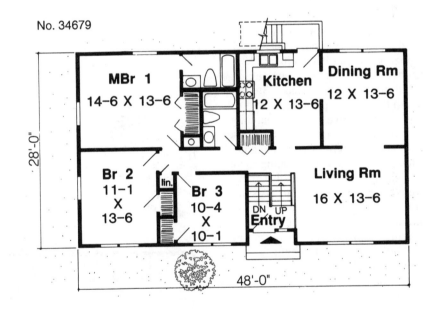

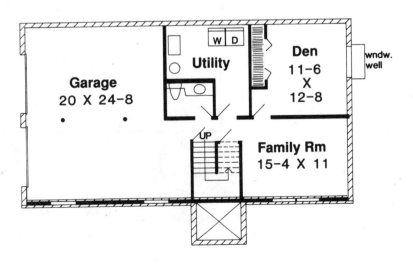

Carefree Convenience

No. 10674

One-level living is a breeze in this attractive, three bedroom beauty designed with your budget in mind. The covered porch adds a romantic touch to the clapboard facade. Step through the front door into a huge living room. Active areas surrounding a spacious patio at the rear of the house are served by a centrally-located galley kitchen. Eat in the formal dining room, or the handy breakfast room that adjoins the huge family room. A short hall leads to a handy full bath and two bedrooms. The master suite, tucked off the living room, features double closets and vanities for early-morning convenience. This plan is built on a slab foundation.

Garage — 465 sq. ft.

Total living area — 1,600 sq. ft.

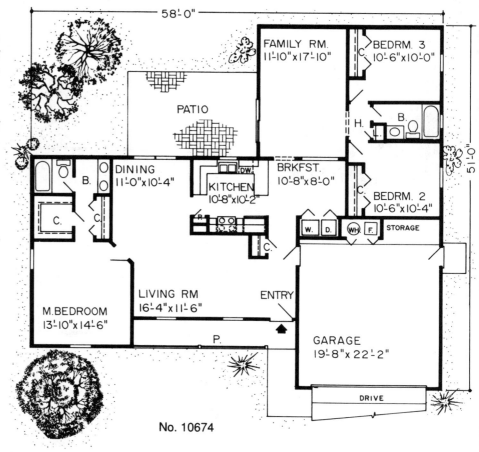

Wide-Open and Convenient

No. 20100

Stacked windows fill the wall in the front bedroom of this one-level home, creating an attractive facade, and a sunny atmosphere inside. Around the corner, two more bedrooms and two full baths complete the bedroom wing, set apart for bedtime quiet. Notice the elegant vaulted-ceiling in the master bedroom, the master tub and shower illuminated by a skylight, and the double vanities in both baths. Active areas enjoy a spacious feeling. Look at the high, sloping ceilings in the fireplaced living room, the sliders that unite the breakfast room and kitchen with an adjoining deck, and the vaulted-ceilings in the formal dining room off the foyer.

Main living area —
1,727 sq. ft.
Basement — 1,727 sq. ft.
Garage — 484 sq. ft.

Total living area —
1,727 sq. ft

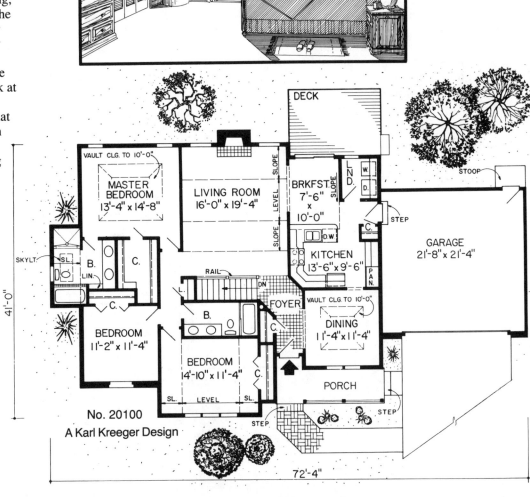

No. 20100
A Karl Kreeger Design

Expansive Two Story Foyer Creates Dramatic Impression

No. 10588

French doors in the breakfast nook give this traditional colonial home a touch of romance. Divided from the kitchen by a peninsula with a counter for informal meals, the breakfast nook is adjacent to the fireplaced family room. Right across the hall, the foyer links living and dining rooms and harbors the angular staircase to four bedrooms and two baths on the second floor.

First floor — 1,450 sq. ft.
Second floor — 1,082 sq. ft.
Basement — 1,340 sq. ft.
Garage — 572 sq. ft.

Total living area — 2,532 sq. ft.

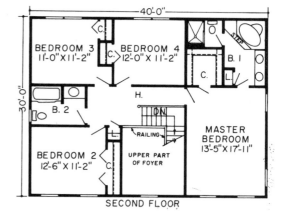

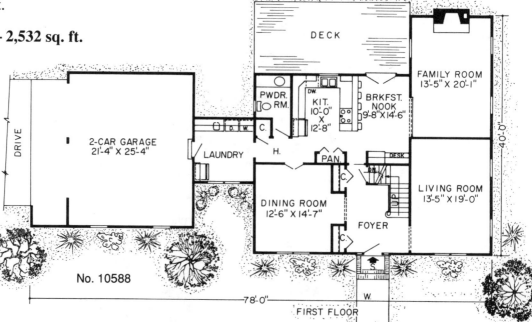

Compact Two Story Has Victorian Flair

No. 90445

This two-story Traditional has room for many residents. The large Great room has a fireplace plus a view of the open stair. The dining room features a boxed window, and leads into the galley-style kitchen. The breakfast nook with bay window is adjacent to the garage and outdoor deck. The guest room with a full bath is perfect for company. Upstairs the master suite has a tray ceiling and convenient media center. The master bath features a corner tub and walk-in closet, as well as a separate shower. Two other bedrooms and another full bath complete the second floor. The optional bonus room over the garage can serve as another bedroom or playroom. The plan is available with either basement, crawlspace or slab foundation. Please specify when ordering.

Main floor — 1,030 sq. ft.
Second floor — 1,020 sq. ft.
Bonus room — 284 sq. ft.

Total living area — 2,050 sq. ft.

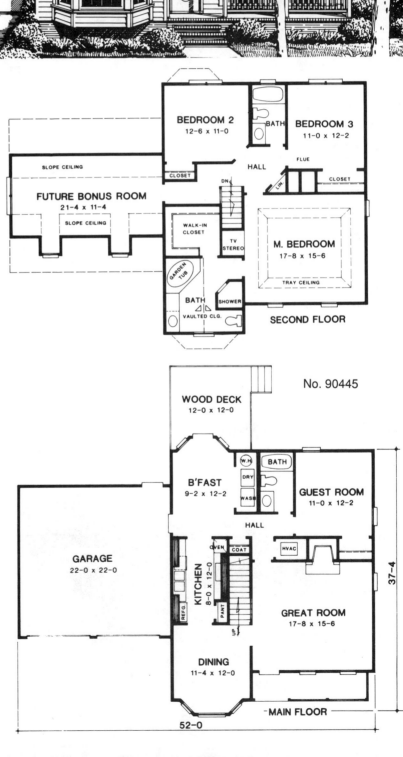

French Country
No. 91658

A pleasant grace surrounds this corner French country dream house. The illuminated foyer, with eighteen-foot ceilings, greets you with formal comfort and access to the dining, den and sunken living room with an arched entry. Through the double French doors is an open family area with the nook and kitchen adjacent, and easy access to the utility room and garage. Upstairs presents an elegant master suite and bath with three spacious bedrooms, a full bath and a large bonus room. All in all, a wonderful place to come home to.

First floor — 1,718 sq. ft.
Second floor — 1,340 sq. ft.
Bonus room — 220 sq. ft.

Total living area — 3,278 sq. ft.

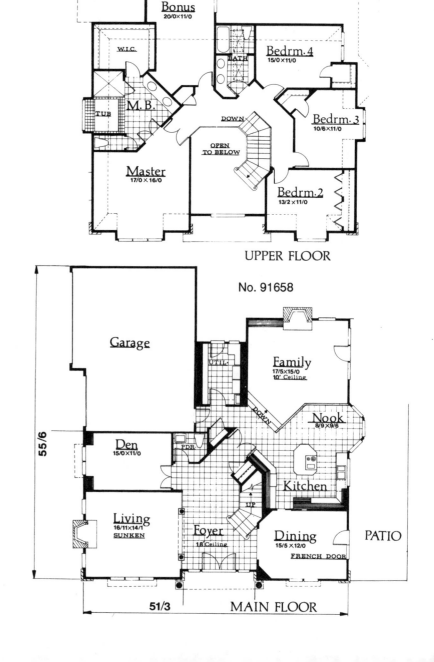

Master Suite Crowns Plan

No. 91650

Tradition on the outside, modern luxury within. The delicate lattice work that covers the entry way, the sheltered porch and the classic lines all recall a bygone era of fine craftmanship. The luxury, that only modern technology can bring, is the theme throughout. From the stately vaulted ceiling of the foyer, up the wide, winding staircase to the apartment-sized master suite, we bring you the finest in modern living. The master suite is the heart of this home, with double doors, spa and a gigantic walk-in closet.

Main floor — 1,288 sq. ft.
Upper floor — 1,094 sq. ft.
Bonus room — 255 sq. ft.

Total living area — 2,637 sq. ft.

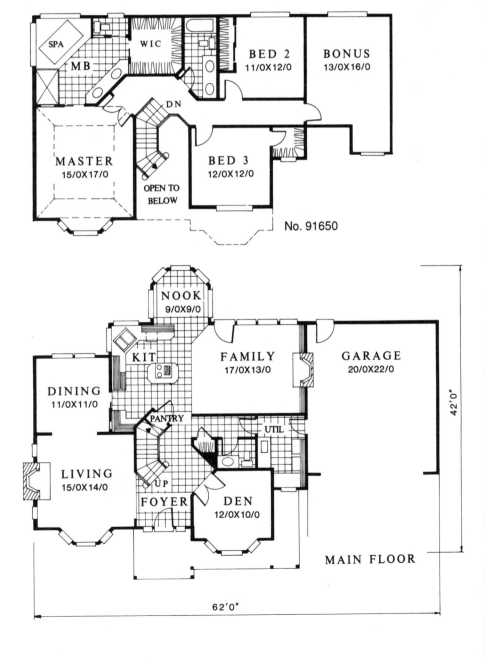

Traditional That Has It All

No. 90443

This one-and-a-half story Traditional offers everything. The plan features a living room for formal affairs, as well as the large Great room for family living. The master suite has two closets, and the bath features corner tub with dual vanities and a separate shower. The large dining room with a bay window is adjacent to the kitchen, which has all major appliances. The breakfast room with bay window is perfect for sunny mornings. The large utility room features space for a freezer and a pantry. Upstairs there are two large bedrooms with walk-in closets. Each bedroom has it's own full bath. The bonus room can be finished as hobby room, office, etc. The mixture of rock and siding, as well as the porch and dormers, give this house a very impressive look from the front. This plan is available with either a basement or crawl space foundation. Please specify when ordering.

First floor — 1,927 sq. ft.
Second floor — 832 sq. ft.
Bonus room — 624 sq. ft.
Basement — 1,674 sq. ft.

Total living area — 2,759 sq. ft.

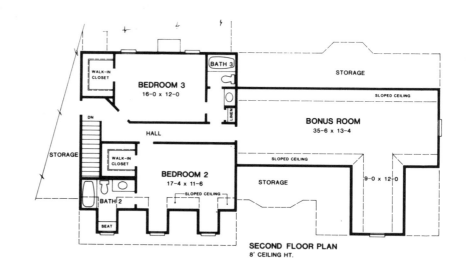

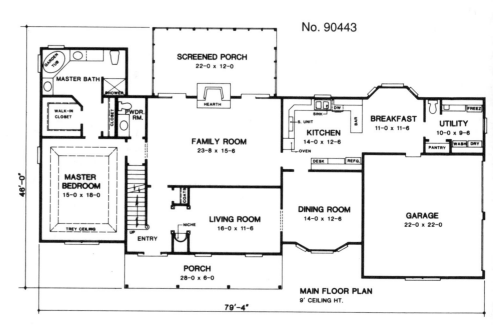

Irresistible Country Charm
No. 92012

A gabled front porch, 1/2 transom glass, and repeating front gables combine to give this plan a taste of country living. The two-story entry offers views through the breakfast to the rear deck area. The first floor den offers the flexibility of office, study, or fourth bedroom. The large island kitchen with breakfast area is open to the family room. Upstairs features two additional bedrooms and bath, and a large master bedroom with his-and-hers walk in closets, a private luxury bath with platform tub, separate shower, and double bowl vanity.

First floor — 1,264 sq. ft.
Second floor — 940 sq. ft.
Basement — 1,252 sq. ft.
Garage — 455 sq. ft.

Total living area — 2,204 sq. ft.

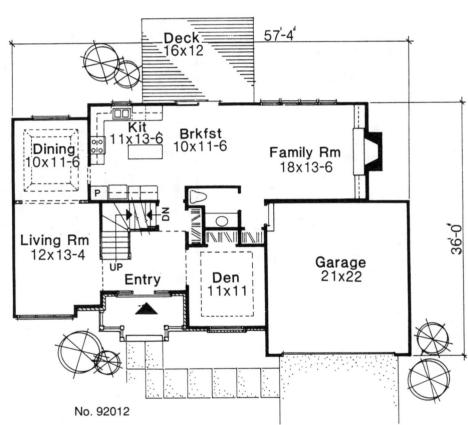

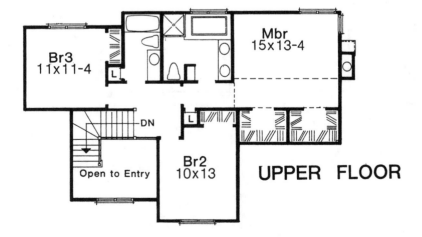

Stucco and Stone Reveal Outstanding Tudor Design

No. 10555

This beautiful stucco and stone masonry Tudor design opens to a formal foyer that leads through double doors into a well-designed library which is also conveniently accessible from the master bedroom. The master bedroom offers a vaulted ceiling and a huge bath area. Other features are an oversized living room with a fireplace, an open kitchen and a connecting dining room. A utility room and half-bath are located next to a two-car garage. One other select option in this design is the separate cedar closet to use for off-season clothes storage.

First floor — 1,671 sq. ft.
Second floor — 505 sq. ft.
Basement — 1,661 sq. ft.
Garage — 604 sq. ft.
Screened porch — 114 sq. ft.

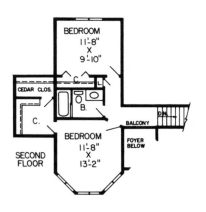

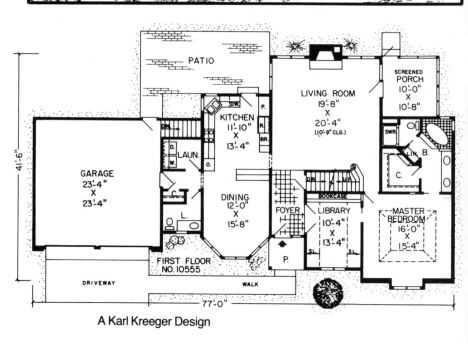

A Karl Kreeger Design

Total living area — 2,176 sq. ft.

Classically Styled

No. 99245

Neo-Georgian styling makes this home a highly visual personal statement for the family moving up with a dramatic pillared entry portico. The inviting master suite upstairs has a balcony overlook to the foyer below, a separate dressing room with built-in vanity, and the huge walk-in closet. Family life is highly convenient with three additional bedrooms and laundry room on the second floor — no more trips to a basement and or even the first floor, carrying awkward clothes baskets. The upstairs lounge will give your children a private space for studying or recreation. Choose the eat-in country kitchen for weekday family meals, with loads of convenient extras. Note the matching built-in china closets in the dining room. Family gatherings and entertainment will be a pleasure in the wonderful ambiance of the Great room with its open space and cozy hearth. The secluded library will be a haven for the family bookworm.

First floor — 1,206 sq. ft.
Second floor — 1,254 sq. ft.
Garage and storage — 378 sq. ft.

Total living area — 2,460 sq. ft.

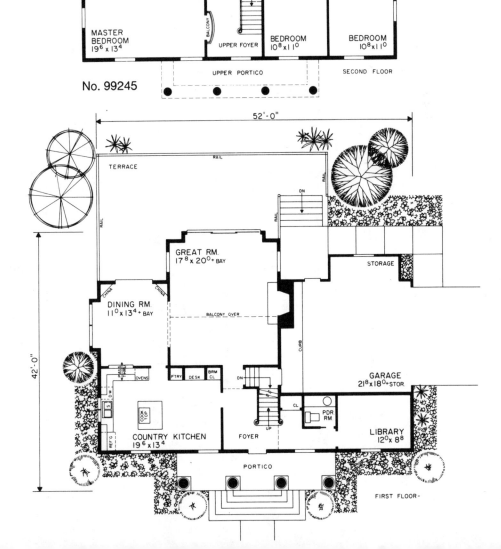

One-Level Living with a Twist

No. 20083

Here's an inviting home with a distinctive difference. Active living areas are wide-open and centrally located. From the foyer, you'll enjoy a full view of the spacious dining, living, and kitchen areas in one sweeping glance. You can even see the deck adjoining the breakfast room. The difference in this house lies in the bedrooms. Each is a private retreat, away from active areas. The master suite at the rear of the house features a full bath with double sinks. Two additional bedrooms, off in their own wing, share a full bath and the quiet atmosphere that results from intelligent design.

First floor — 1,575 sq. ft.
Basement — 1,575 sq. ft.
Garage — 475 sq. ft.

Total living area — 1,575 sq. ft.

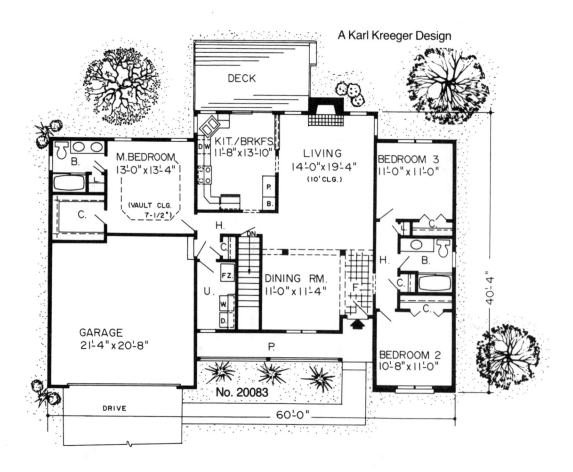

Adaptable For the Disabled
No. 91652

The charming and cozy exterior of this two-plus bedroom, two bath home does not prepare you for the drama within. Elegant arched doorways lead you to the living and family rooms. Entertain in the dining room, warm up to a cozy fireplace or study in the den; comfort abounds in every room of this warm home. Designed as a lifetime home, it is handicap accessible and has convenient, luxurious features such as an expansive kitchen with walk-in pantry and breakfast nook, and a large walk-in closet in the master bedroom.

Main living area — 1,541 sq. ft.
Garage — 2-car

Total living area — 1,541 sq. ft.

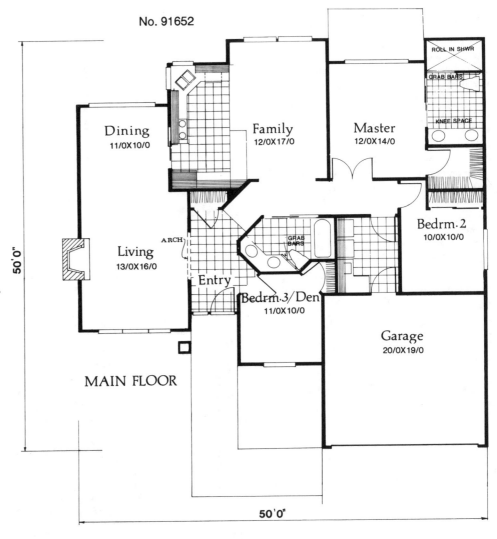

Colonial Charmer Fit for a Crowd

No. 20101

Imagine entertaining in this spacious masterpiece! Throw open the double doors between the front parlor and fireplaced family room and you've got an expansive room that can handle any crowd. There's room for an army of cooks in the bayed kitchen/breakfast room combination. In addition, store extra supplies in the spacious pantry on the way to the elegant, formal dining room. The adjacent breezeway contains a handy powder room and laundry facilities. Four bedrooms are tucked upstairs, away from the action. Look at the magnificent master suite. Recessed ceilings, a skylit shower, and double vanities make this room both luxurious and convenient.

First floor — 1,109 sq. ft.
Second floor — 932 sq. ft.
Basement — 1,109 sq. ft.
Garage — 552 sq. ft.

Total living area — 2,041 sq. ft.

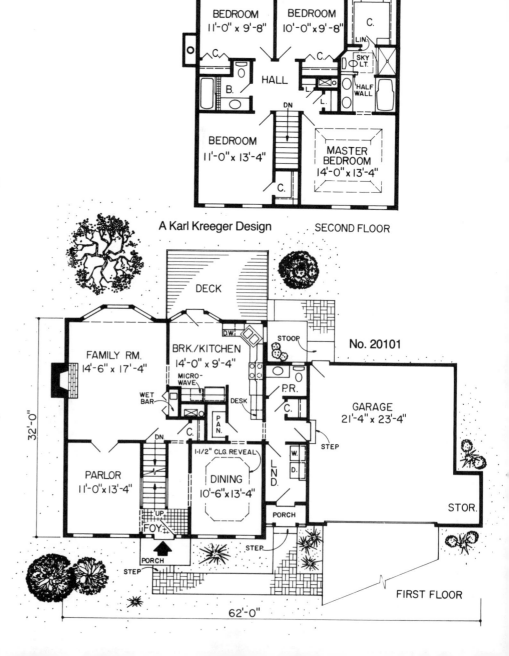

Appeal Everyone Wants

No. 92016

This house will surely turn heads with its repeating front gables, shuttered windows, and wrap-around front porch. Just pass through the entry and be treated to a long view to the corner glass and fireplace conversation area in the Great room. The large family/kitchen opens to a screened porch and private side deck. The rear located open stair offers a privacy you can't get with entry stair cases. Upstairs you will find a large master bedroom with private bath, a second bath, two additional bedrooms, and laundry facilities.

First floor — 760 sq. ft.
Second floor — 728 sq. ft.
Basement — 768 sq. ft.
Garage — 407 sq. ft.

Total living area — 1,488 sq. ft.

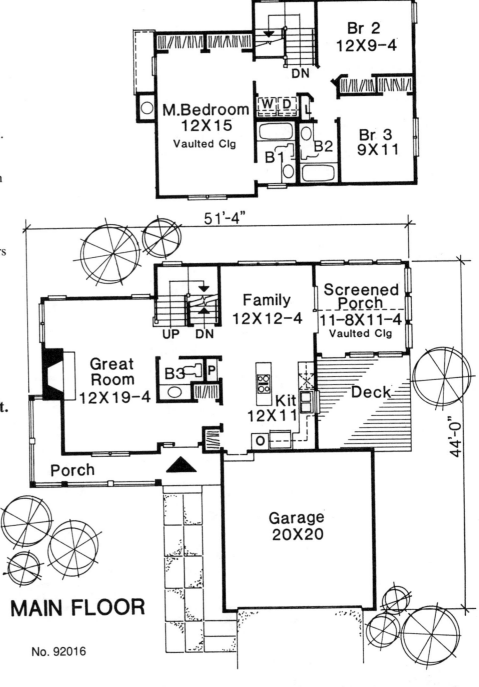

MAIN FLOOR

No. 92016

Elegant and Inviting
No. 10689

Traditional and modern elements unite to create an outstanding plan for the family that enjoys outdoor entertaining. Wrap-around verandas and a three-season porch insure the party will stay dry, rain or shine. You may want to keep guests inside, in the elegant parlor and formal dining room, separated by a half-wall. The adjoining kitchen can be closed off to keep meal preparation convenient, but removed from the bustle. The family will enjoy informal meals at the island bar, or in the adjoining breakfast nook. Even the fireplaced gathering room, with its soaring ceilings and access to the porch, is right nearby. You'll appreciate the first floor master suite, and the upstairs laundry location.

First floor — 1,580 sq. ft.
Second floor — 1,164 sq. ft.
Basement — 1,329 sq. ft.
Garage — 576 sq. ft.

Total living area — 2,744 sq. ft.

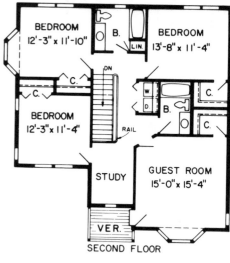

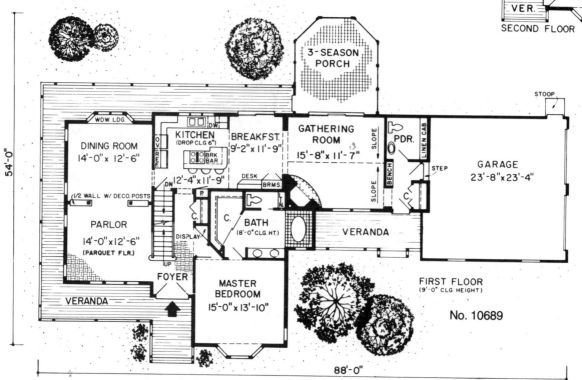

Bridge Over Foyer Introduces Unique Features

No. 10535

A dynamic foyer opens into a cathedral-ceilinged Great room, complete with a cozy fireplace framed on both sides with bookshelves. The unique octagonal breakfast nook is tucked into a spacious kitchen with a view of the backyard. The master bedroom boasts a quaint, but roomy, sitting room. Three full baths and two half baths are conveniently located for family and guests.

First floor — 2,335 sq. ft.
Second floor — 1,157 sq. ft.
Basement — 2,281 sq. ft.
Garage — 862 sq. ft.

Total living area — 3,492 sq. ft.

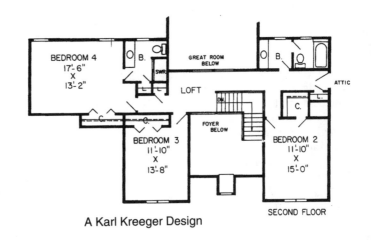

A Karl Kreeger Design

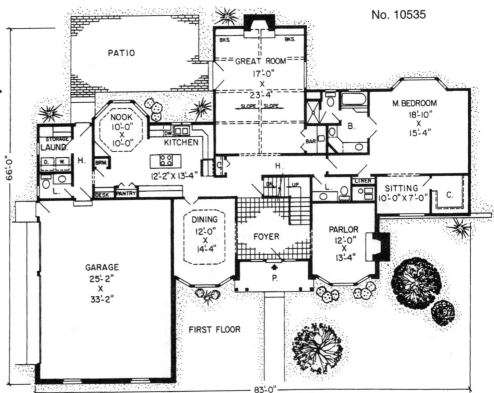

Modest Tudor with a Massive Look

No. 90012

Specifically designed to make its presence felt in any neighborhood, this stately Tudor home contains fewer square feet, and is more affordable, than one would imagine. Broken and steeply sloping roof lines, dormers, a large cantilevered bay, and a unique Gothic shaped entrance —as well as the charming stone, brick, and half-timber materials— all add keen interest to the exterior. The living-dining space is an open 34 ft. area designed to be an impressive focal point; a large log-burning fireplace is centrally located on the far wall. The triple windows in the front allow for a grand view.

First floor — 1,078 sq. ft.
Second floor — 1,131 sq. ft.
Garage — 2-car

Total living area — 2,209 sq. ft.

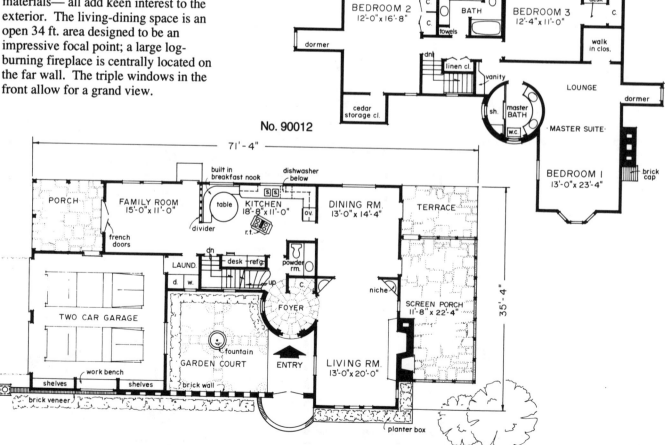

Double Doors Give Spanish Welcome

No. 10108

Massive double doors open to the foyer of this multi-arched Spanish design and balance three sets of double doors opening to a second floor balcony. Spanning over 27 feet, the living room occupies the entire area to the right of the foyer, while the kitchen and family room edge the left side. Hallway, bath, and laundry niche separate the areas and buffer noises. Three large bedrooms boast two baths.

First floor — 1,176 sq. ft.
Second floor — 1,176 sq. ft.
Basement — 1,176 sq. ft.
Garage — 576 sq. ft.

Total living area — 2,352 sq. ft.

No. 10108

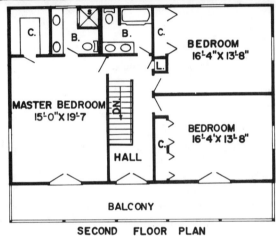

Compact Ranch Loaded with Living Space

No. 34328

A central entry opens to a spacious living room with ample windows and a handy closet nearby. The kitchen features a dining area with sliding glass doors to the backyard and optional deck. A hallway separates three bedrooms and a full bath from the active areas. The laundry facilities are tucked behind double doors for slab/crawlspace options.

Main living area — 1,092 sq. ft.
Basement — 1,092 sq. ft.

Total living area — 1,092 sq. ft.

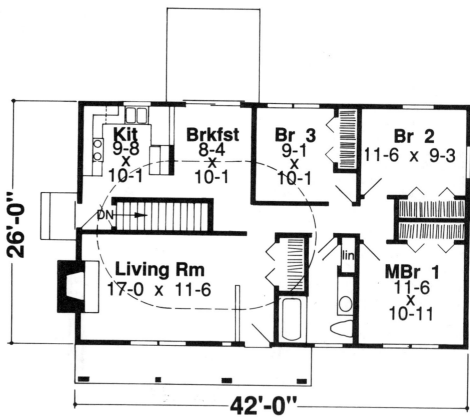

No. 34328

ALTERNATE FLOOR PLAN for Crawl Space

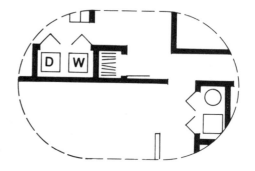

Ranch Provides Great Kitchen Area

No. 34054

There's a lot of convenience packed into this affordable design. Flanking the kitchen to the right is the dining room which has a sliding glass door to the backyard, and to the left is the laundry room with an entrance to the garage. The master bedroom boasts its own full bathroom and the additional two bedrooms share the hall bath. An optional two-car garage plan is included.

Main living area — 1,400 sq. ft.
Basement — 1,400 sq. ft.
Garage — 528 sq. ft.

Total living area — 1,400 sq. ft.

Alternate Plan w/ Crawlspace

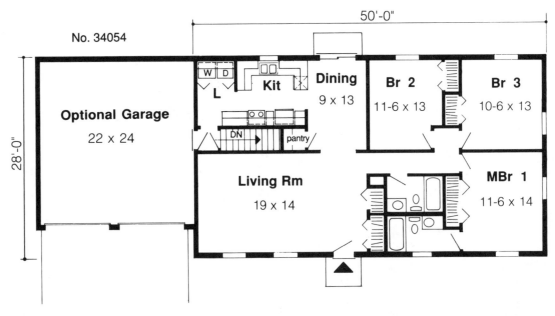

Small Scale, Lots of Space

No. 90390

Here's an attractive, one-level plan that's a good value for the family on a budget. This compact design uses corner windows and vaulted ceilings, eliminating unnecessary walls for an airy feeling throughout active areas. A corner fireplace adds interesting angles and a toasty atmosphere to the living room. The cook in the house will appreciate the close proximity of the kitchen to the dining room. Three bedrooms, tucked at the rear of the house for privacy, are served by two full baths. And, the master suite features the same angular interest and corner window treatment that makes the living room so sunny and spacious.

Main living area — 1,231 sq. ft.
Garage — 2-car

Total living area — 1,231 sq. ft.

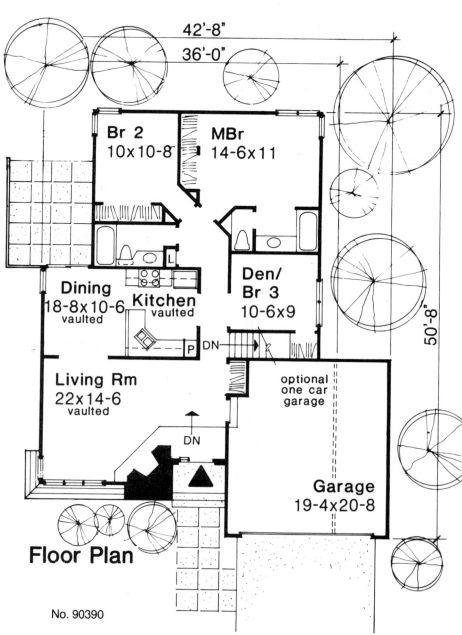

No. 90390

Easy Access; Easy Living

No. 99338

The living and dining rooms access a large deck, inviting outdoor meals and entertaining. The massive fireplace is flanked on each side by windows creating spectacular landscape views. A columned arcade divides living and dining areas. The bedroom off the front entrance might serve well as a den or office. The vaulted master suite includes walk-in wardrobe, luxurious spa bathing, and access to the deck.

Main living area — 1,642 sq. ft.
Basement — 1,642 sq. ft.
Garage — 2-car

Total living area — 1,642 sq. ft.

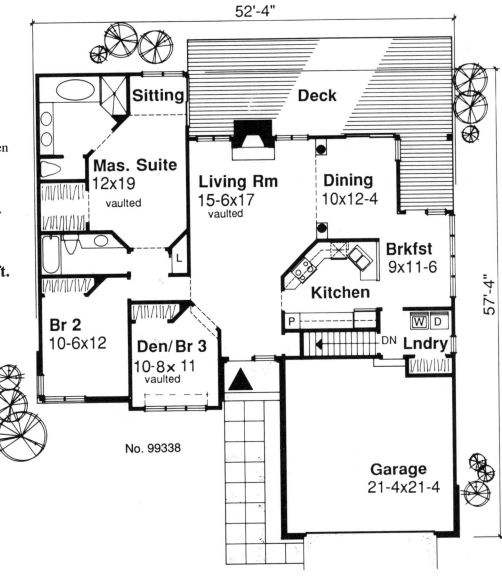

Traditional Ranch Has Many Modern Features

No. 90444

This Ranch plan is ideal for a corner lot, with a rear garage that enters from the side. The focal point of this plan is the Great room with a vaulted ceiling, and loft above. The French doors on either side of the fireplace open onto a screened porch. The large double-L kitchen is open to the breakfast room, which has a bay window. The master bedroom has a large walk-in closet, and the master bath features a corner tub, as well as double vanities. Two other bedrooms on the opposite end of the house make this split-bedroom design popular. Each of these bedrooms has a walk-in closet, and a desk for school-age children. The loft has a vaulted-ceiling and overlooks the Great room with an open rail balcony. This plan is available with either a basement or crawl space foundation. Please specify when ordering.

Main floor — 1,996 sq. ft.
Loft — 305 sq. ft.

Total living area — 2,301 sq. ft.

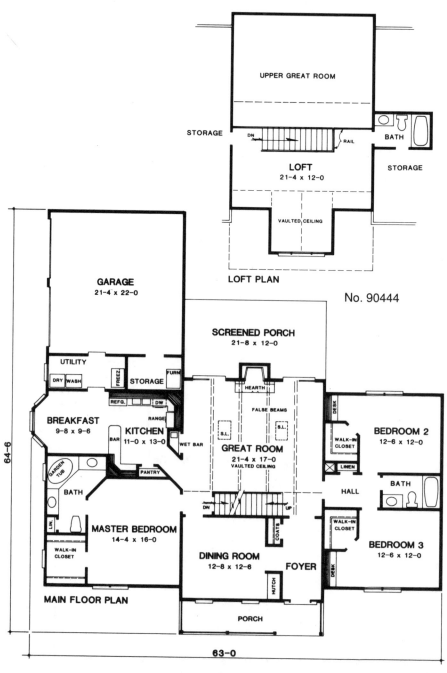

For The Young At Heart

No. 99324

For the move-down buyers on the go or the family on the grow, this three bedroom home has all the right features. The home draws its look from the nostalgic elements of older traditional homes. It has half-round transom and gable details, divided light windows, covered entry porch and bay windows. The interior features a vaulted Great room with fireplace and transom window, and a vaulted kitchen with breakfast area and sliders to the deck. The master suite has its own bath.

Main living area — 1,307 sq. ft.
Garage — 2-car

Total living area — 1,307 sq. ft

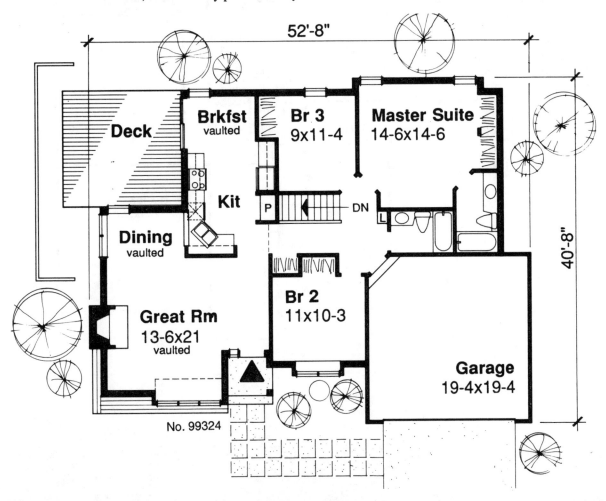

Luxurious Master Suite Highlights Plan

No. 91645

As you round the bend, home at last after another hectic day at the office, you see the setting sun reflected in the crystal-clear living room windows, bathing the brick highlights in a golden splendor. You walk in and shake the worries of yet another day from your shoulders. Stopping for a moment in the spacious kitchen to pour yourself a drink and head for the invigorating embrace of your very own spa. "Yes", you say as you dim the lights, "Success is definitely worth the price!"

Main living area — 1,998 sq. ft.

Total living area — 1,998 sq. ft.

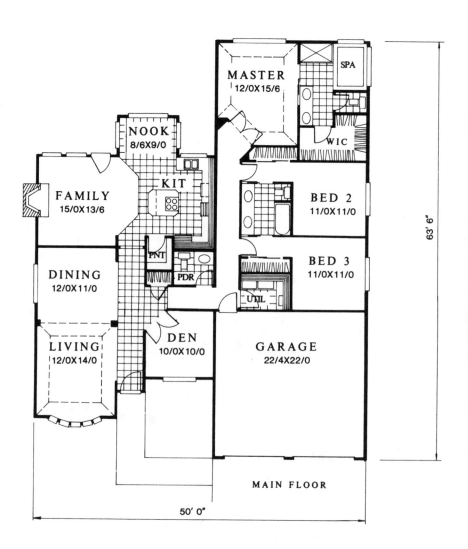

No. 91645

Quaint Starter Home

No. 92400

This delightful 1,050 sq. ft. plan is designed as a "starter" home or "empty-nester". It also lends itself well to a vacation atmosphere. A vaulted ceiling gives an airy feeling to the dining and living areas. The streamline kitchen has a comfortable work triangle. A cozy fireplace makes the living area really feel like home. The master suite has a large closet, a French door leading onto a patio and a spacious master bath. The two remaining bedrooms share a hall bath. The washer and dryer are tucked conveniently in a laundry closet.

Main living area — 1,050 sq. ft.
Garage — 1-car

Total living area — 1,050 sq. ft.

No materials list available

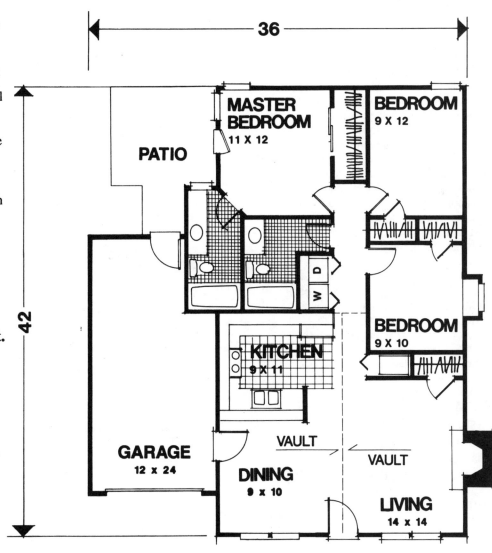

National Treasure

No. 24400

This delightful home's wrap-around covered porch recalls the warmth and charm of days past — lounging in the porch swing, savoring life. Inside, a spacious foyer welcomes guests and provides easy access to the formal dining room, secluded den/guest room (which might serve as your home office), and the large living room. Ceilings downstairs are all 9' high, with decorative vaults in the living and dining rooms. The kitchen, with its island/breakfast bar, is large enough for two people to work in comfortably. The adjacent laundry room also serves as a mud room for boots and clothes, and leads directly to the garage, which features an ample storage/shop area at the rear. Upstairs, three bedrooms, each with cathedral ceilings, share a cheery, sunlit sitting area that also features a cathedral ceiling. For privacy, the master bedroom is separated from the other bedrooms, and boasts a palatial bathroom, complete with a whirlpool tub. If room to relax is what you're after, this home is loaded with irresistible features.

First floor — 1,034 sq. ft.
Second floor — 944 sq. ft.
Basement — 944 sq. ft.
Garage & Storage — 684 sq. ft.

Total living area — 1,978 sq. ft.

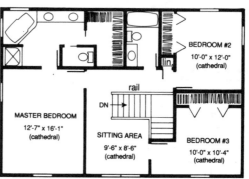

Second Floor

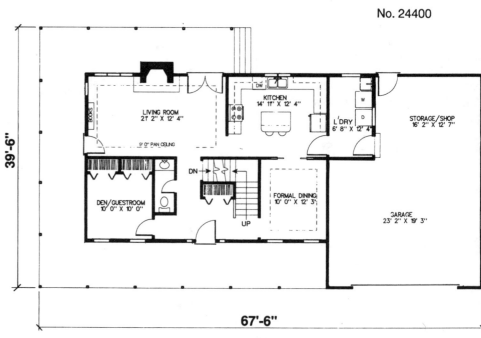

First Floor

Compact Ranch

No. 99345

Compact and comfortable living is featured in this lovely three bedroom ranch. Enter into an open Great room and dining area with vaulted ceilings. Included in the Great room is a fabulous fireplace, benefitted by both those relaxing on the sofa or those enjoying a candlelit dinner. The kitchen and sunny breakfast area, also with vaulted ceiling, have access to a wonderfully delightful rear deck. The master suite is furnished with its own private full bath. Two other bedrooms sharing a separate bathroom, complete this home.

First floor — 1,325 sq. ft.
Garage — 2-car

Total living area — 1,325 sq. ft.

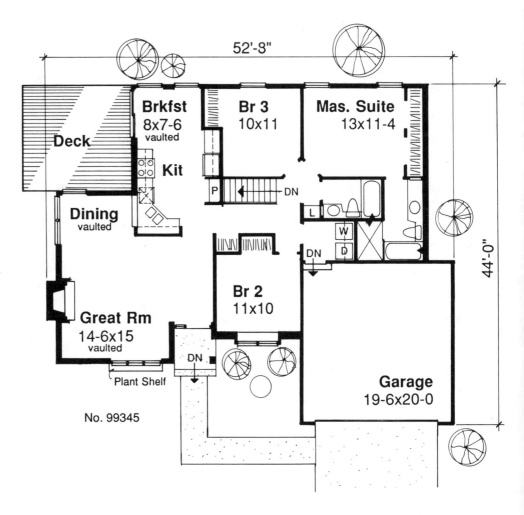

First Floor Master Suite

No. 24316

As you enter this home the elevated foyer directs entry traffic into the formal living areas or the family room beyond. The living room receives natural light through the large front window. The formal dining room is located next to the kitchen making serving this room simple and easy. The modern, efficient kitchen offers a corner double basin sink, bay area for informal eating and easy access to the patio through the door in the family room. The family room has a fantastic corner fireplace to serve as its focal point. This large room is sure to please your family's needs. The master suite located on this floor insures privacy, since all the other bedrooms are upstairs. The private master bath has separate shower and oval tub. Bedroom three enjoys a walk-in closet and they all share a full hall bath.

First floor — 1,400 sq. ft.
Second floor — 540 sq. ft.

Total living area — 1,940 sq. ft.

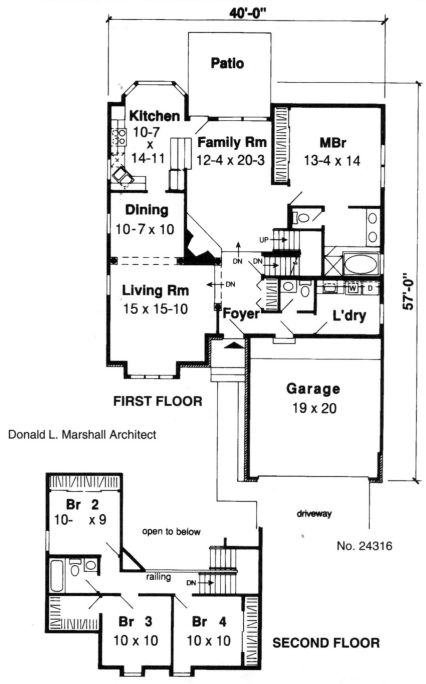

Skylight Brightens Breakfast Nook

No. 24251

A covered porch welcomes your visitor to your home. Upon entering your visitor will enjoy dining in your vaulted ceiling formal dining room with inviting bay window. The living room adjoins the dining room making transition in entertaining easy. You will enjoy your center island kitchen. Its efficient use of space, double basin sink and numerous amenities makes your life convenient. The sunny, skylighted breakfast nook is a cheerful start to your day. The family room has a fireplace with built-in bookshelves or entertainment center. Notice the wetbar. It is convenient to both the formal and informal entertainment areas. The second floor offers a master suite with cathedral ceiling, walk-in closet and private bath with separate shower and tub. The secondary bedrooms share a full hall bath.

First floor — 707 sq. ft.
Second floor — 907 sq. ft.

Total living area — 1,614 sq. ft.

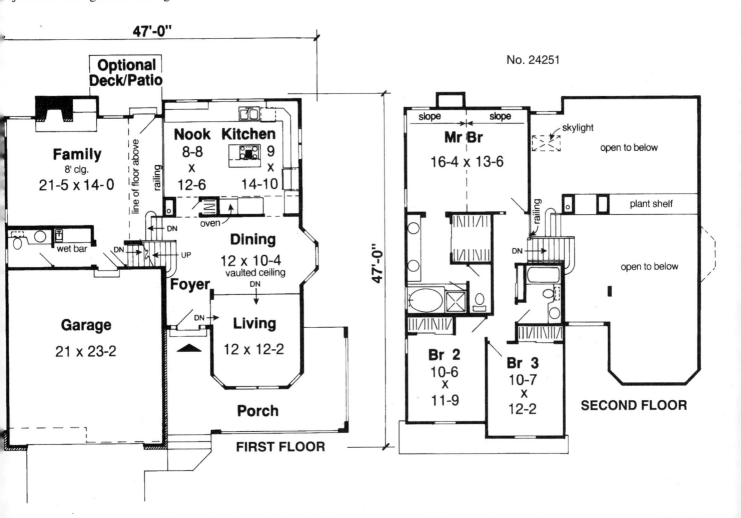

Watch the World Go By

No. 90157

Two porches adorn the facade of this country charmer with two-story entry foyer. Upstairs, the wrap-around balcony leads to four ample bedrooms, including the master suite with corner platform tub. The front bedroom boasts vaulted ceilings and an oversized, half-round window. A huge family room with fireplace and built-in shelves opens to a rear patio and to the breakfast nook and family kitchen. This plan can be built with a basement, slab or crawl space foundation. Please specify when ordering.

First floor — 1,428 sq. ft.
Second floor — 1,369 sq. ft.

Total living area — 2,797 sq. ft.

SECOND FLOOR

No. 90157

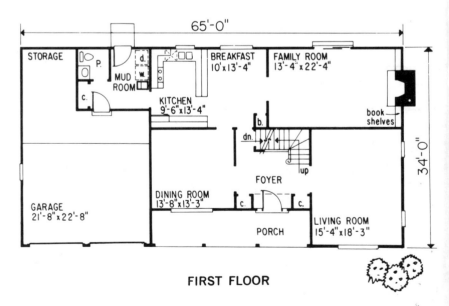

FIRST FLOOR

Traditional Warmth with a Modern Accent

No. 10638

Gracious touches make this spacious dwelling a place you'll love to come home to. Look at the recessed ceilings in the living, dining, and master bedrooms. Rustic beams, a cozy fireplace, and built-in shelves make the family room special. Notice the efficient placement of kitchen and utility areas adjacent to formal and informal dining rooms. With four bedrooms upstairs, this is a perfect family home. You can watch the kids playing on the patio from the cozy bay-windowed sitting nook in the master suite.

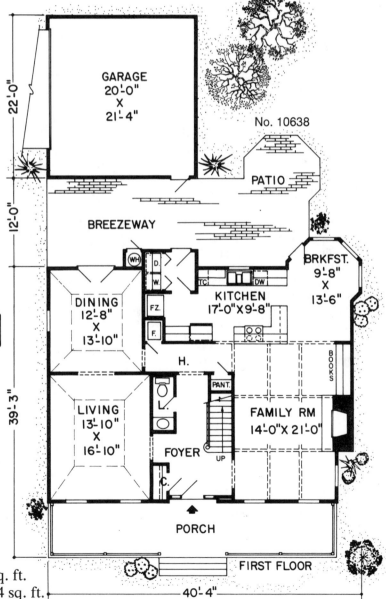

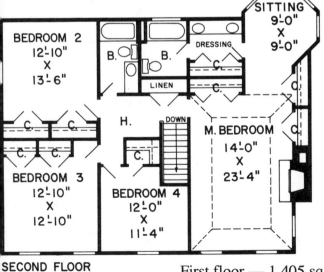

First floor — 1,405 sq. ft.
Second floor — 1,364 sq. ft.
Garage — 458 sq. ft.

Total living area — 2,769 sq. ft.

Rambling Ranch

No. 24314

This rambling Ranch offers you the convenience of one floor living. From the foyer you have easy access to the living room. The focal point fireplace attracts your attention as does the custom ceiling treatment. The dining room is also enhanced by a custom ceiling. The modern kitchen has access to both the dining and the family room. The master bedroom boasts a private master bath with separate shower and oval tub. The large walk-in closet allows for ample storage. The secondary bedrooms share a full hall bath. The entry from the garage allows for easy bathroom access, keeping the rest of the home clean. The family room and the master bedroom have access to the outside. The convenience of one floor living, isn't it for you?

Main living area — 1,850 sq. ft.

Total living area — 1,850 sq. ft.

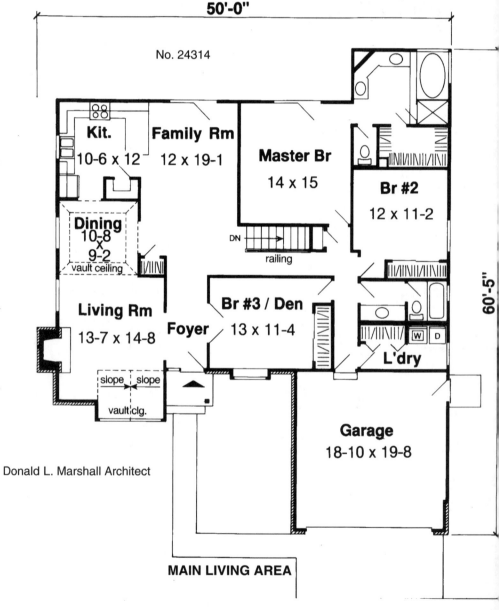

Donald L. Marshall Architect

Clever Design Packs in Plenty of Living Space

No. 24250

The design of this home allows for plenty of living space. This home makes use of custom, volume ceilings. The living room offers a sunk-in environment. The vaulted ceiling and fireplace give this room drama. The oversized windows framing the fireplace enhance the drama with natural light. The kitchen features a center island and eating nook. There is more than ample counter space, plus a double basin sink and all the amenities you could ask for. The formal dining room adjoins the kitchen allowing for easy entertaining. The spacious master suite enjoys a vaulted ceiling. Its lavish master bath allows for privacy and pampering. Cozy, comfortable, and peaceful are the feelings you get as you curl up on the window seat on a rainy afternoon to read your book. This suite is your own private get-away. The secondary bedrooms also have custom ceiling treatments and large windows that view the front porch.

Main living area — 1,700 sq. ft.

Total living area — 1,700 sq. ft.

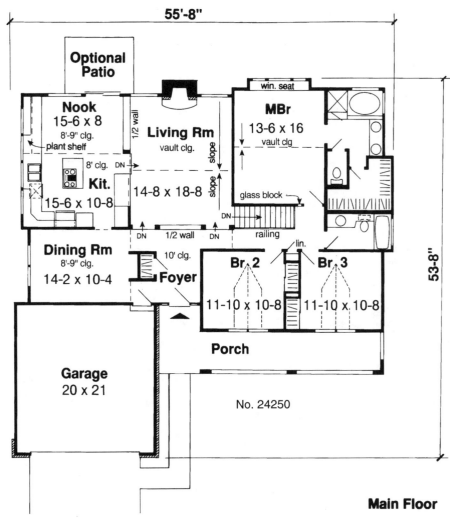

Main Floor

A Winning Combination

No. 99326

Old world traditional appeal, plus modern design concepts combine to make this a stunning 3,042 square foot luxury design. The interior offers dramatic features at every turn, beginning with the living room with a vaulted ceiling and loft overlook accessible by the angled stair tower. The formal dining room has a tray ceiling and looks out over the rear yard deck. The island kitchen is the heart of the informal living area of the home. The second floor master suite is stunning with its vaulted ceiling and fireplace. Two more bedrooms on this floor complete the plan.

Main floor — 1,636 sq. ft.
Upper floor — 1,406 sq. ft.
Garage — 2-car

Total living area — 3,042 sq. ft

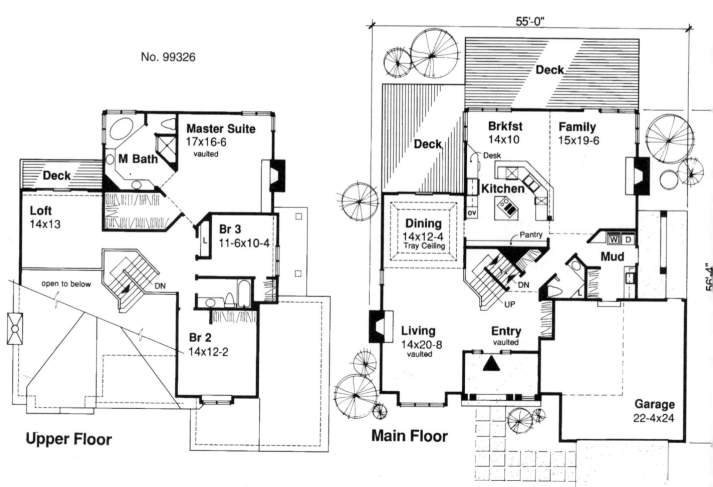

Students Love the Alcove

No. 91351

Starting at the sheltered entry, this home with its many appealing features, lends itself well to those desiring comfortable family living. The well planned layout is ideal for today's growing family. This single level traditional styled home has a total of 1,477 sq. ft. and there are two distinctive elevations from which to choose. The entry opens to the living room that is enhanced by a stone hearth fireplace. It flows into the dining room, with built-in shelves, or to the family room, open to the efficiently designed kitchen. The master bedroom suite is complete with walk-in closet, double sink vanity, and a private shower. Bedrooms two and three are served by a full bath located in the hall. Note the study alcove in bedroom number three. The efficient compact laundry room leads to the double car garage that also has a side entry door. A porch at the rear of the house is perfect for entertaining, and can be accessed from either the master bedroom suite or the family room.

Main living area — 1,477 sq. ft.
Garage — 2-car

Total living area — 1,477 sq. ft.

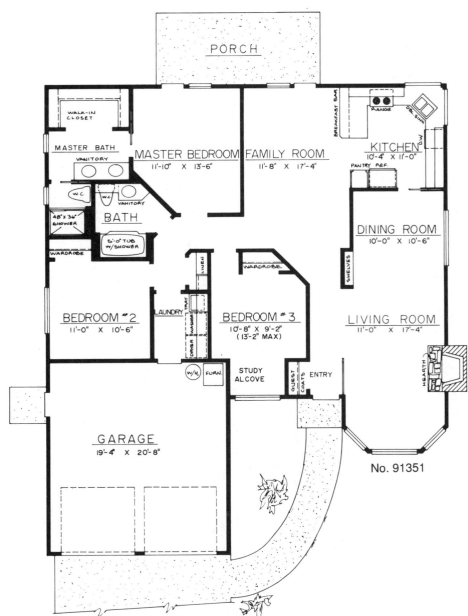

A Hint of Victorian Nostalgia

No. 90909

High roofs, tower bays, and long, railed porches give this efficient plan an old-fashioned charm that's hard to resist. The foyer opens on a classic center stairwell, wrapped in short halls that separate traffic without subtracting from room sizes. The highlight of this home for many homeowners is sure to be the lively kitchen with its full bay window and built-in eating table.

Main floor — 1,206 sq. ft.
Second floor — 969 sq. ft.
Unfinished basement — 1,206 sq. ft.
Garage — 471 sq. ft.
Width — 61'-0"
Depth — 44'-0"

Total living area —2,175 sq. ft.

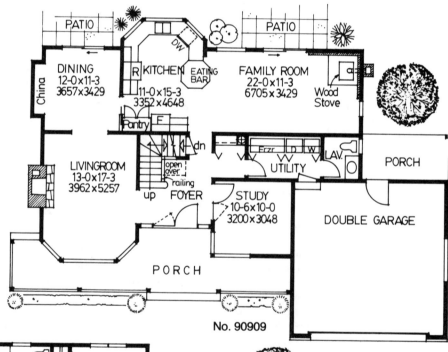

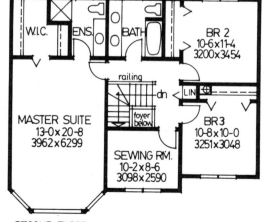

SECOND FLOOR

Two-Sink Baths Ease Rush

No. 90622

Save energy and construction costs by building this friendly farmhouse Colonial. The inviting covered porch opens to a center hall, enhanced by the stairway leading to the four-bedroom second floor. Flanked by formal living and dining rooms, the foyer leads right into the open-beamed family room, island kitchen and bay windowed dinette. The rear porch adjoins both family and living rooms.

First floor — 983 sq. ft.
Second floor — 1,013 sq. ft.
Mudroom — 99 sq. ft.
Garage — 481 sq. ft.

Total living area — 2,095 sq. ft.

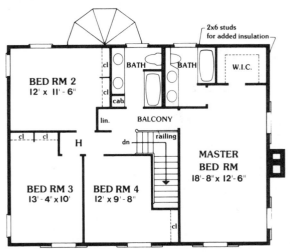

SECOND FLOOR PLAN

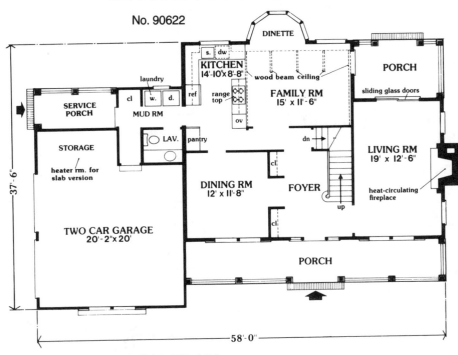

FIRST FLOOR PLAN

Distinctive Bays

No. 24551

The distinctive bay windows highlight this home. As you enter, you can't help noticing the open-rail staircase rising from the elevated foyer to the second floor. Located on your left is the formal living room, with natural light streaming in from the bay window. To your right is the formal dining room, also complemented by a bay window. The island kitchen extends into the spacious breakfast bay. A bright and sunny way to start your morning. The family room features a central fireplace for cozy winter nights of family togetherness. The second floor loft includes built-in bookshelves and an enchanting window seat. The magnificent master suite has a dramatic cathedral ceiling and lavish master bath. The three secondary bedrooms have ample closet space and share a full compartmented hall bath with a double basin vanity and linen closet.

First floor — 1,324 sq. ft.
Second floor — 1,216 sq. ft.

Total living area — 2,540 sq. ft.

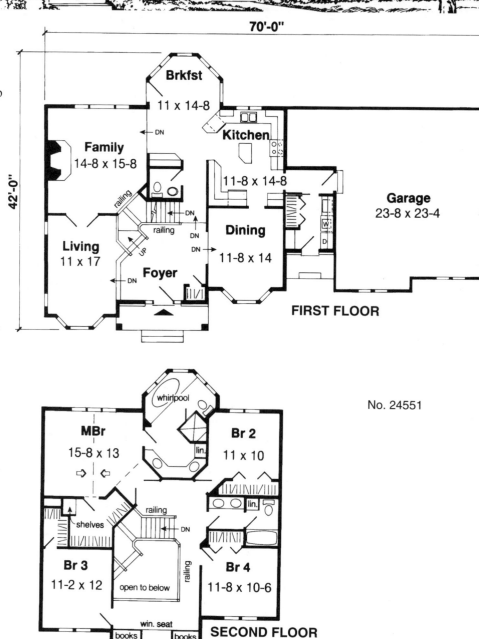

Impressive Brick

No. 24550

This impressive brick home's decorative use of brick detailing around the windows creates a home with abundant curb appeal. The living room features a dramatic cathedral ceiling and a two-way fireplace. This room enjoys the natural light from the large front window. The dining room is complemented by a bay window. The fireplace in the family room adjoins a built-in entertainment center. This room is sure to be the hub of family life in the home. Notice the oversized kitchen island which can easily double as a snack bar. The kitchen boasts a pantry and built-in desk as well as ample cabinet and counter space. The second floor has four bedrooms. The master suite has a vaulted ceiling, walk-in closet and luxurious master bath. The secondary bedrooms have ample closet space and share a hall full bath with dual basin vanity and linen closet. This is truly a home to be proud of.

First floor — 1,428 sq. ft.
Second floor — 1,248 sq. ft.

Total living area — 2,676 sq. ft.

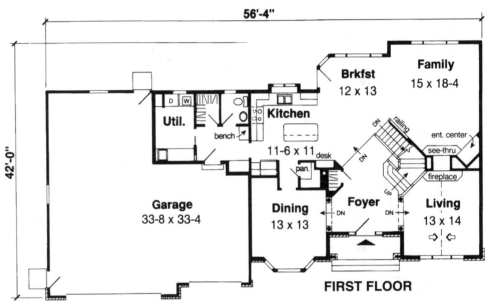

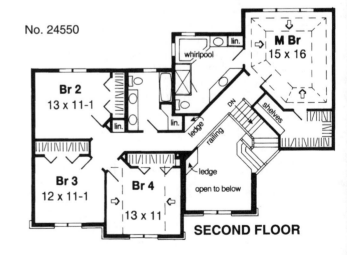

Enticing Two-Story Traditional

No. 34027

This beautiful home accommodates the needs of a growing family and looks stunning in any neighborhood. The porch serves as a wonderful, relaxing area to enjoy the outdoors. As well, in the back is a patio, for a barbeque or for more private time away from the kids. Inside is just as delightful. The dining room features a decorative ceiling and has easy entry to the kitchen. The kitchen/utility area has a side exit into the garage. The living room has double doors into the fireplaced family room which features a back entrance to the patio. Upstairs is the sleeping area with three bedrooms plus a vaulted-ceiling master bedroom. The master bedroom has two enormous walk-in closets, as well as a dressing area and private bath. Please indicate slab, crawl space or basement when ordering.

First floor — 925 sq. ft.
Second floor — 975 sq. ft.
Garage — 484 sq. ft.

Total living area — 1,900 sq. ft.

A Karl Kreeger Design

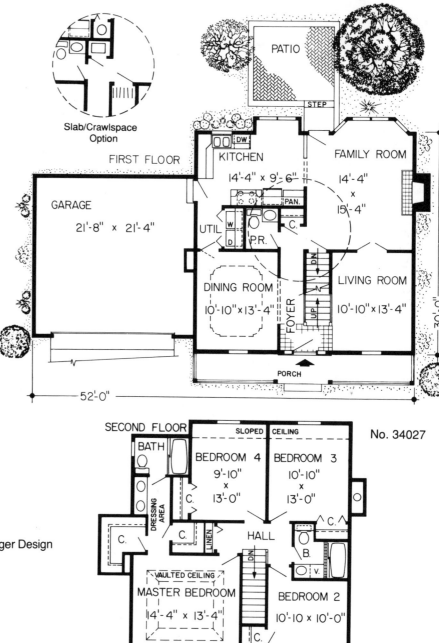

Energy Efficient

No. 90130

Choose either a single or double garage to complement this compact, three bedroom plan. Lots of living is packed into this space conscious design which is organized around the multi-purpose Great room. This extra large living area accommodates all of the family's activities by making the galley-style kitchen an integral part of the living space. Another advantage of the room arrangement is seen in the separation of the living area from the three bedrooms. This separation is achieved through the placement of the two full baths and of the closets. Specify basement or crawl space when ordering.

Main living area — 1,118 sq. ft.

Total living area — 1,118 sq. ft.

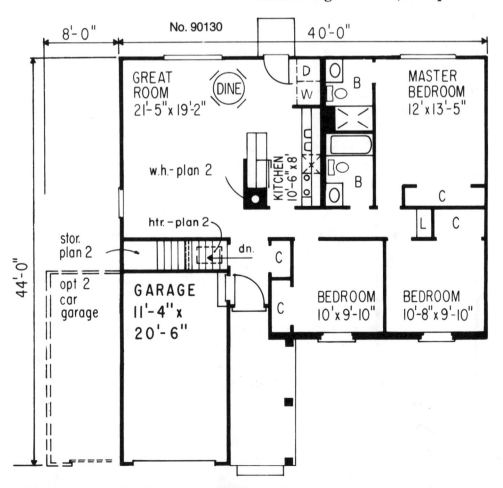

Zoned for Privacy

No. 90673

Here's a contemporary charmer that combines one-story convenience with energy-saving solar features. To the right of the central foyer, ingenious placement of baths and closets shields the three bedrooms from the bustle of active areas. The huge living room, dining room, and kitchen share a wide-open feeling, thanks to huge expanses of glass and skylit cathedral ceilings.

Double your warm-weather living space by opening the sliders in the living room, dining room, and master suite to the wrap-around deck that extends the full length of the house. And, when the nights get cool, you'll appreciate the energy savings from a heat-circulating fireplace and two-by-six construction.

Main living area — 1,324 sq. ft.
Garage — 266 sq. ft.

Total living area — 1,324 sq. ft.

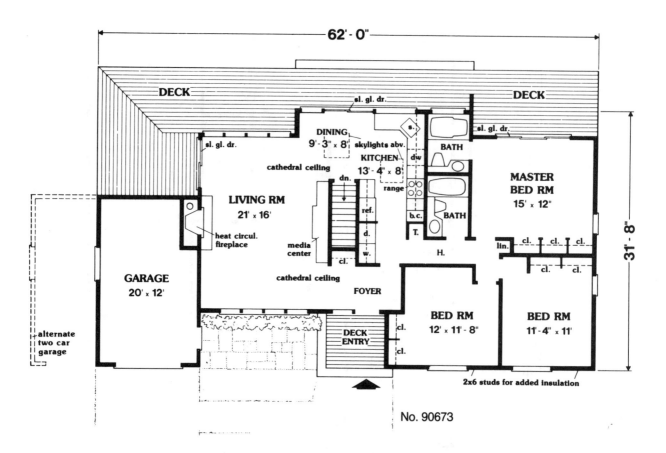

Visual Excitement

No. 90665

Here's an exciting home built for beautiful views inside and out. Standing on the bridge that connects the two upstairs bedrooms and full bath, you can survey your two-story foyer, the sunken living room, and even the rear patio that lies beyond the double sliding glass doors. The view from the dining room is just as exciting. The bow window brings the outdoors inside. And, the brick wall surrounding the fireplace in the adjoining sunken living room rises two stories to a dizzying height. Beauty isn't the only asset possessed by this magnificent home. The convenience of the kitchen to both dining areas, the handy lavatory for your guests, and the quiet repose of a separate bedroom wing are all the result of an ingenious plan with the homeowner in mind.

First floor — 1,458 sq. ft.
Second floor — 470 sq. ft.

Total living area — 1,928 sq. ft.

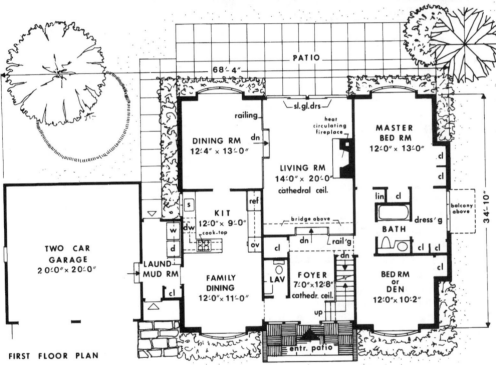

FIRST FLOOR PLAN

No. 90665

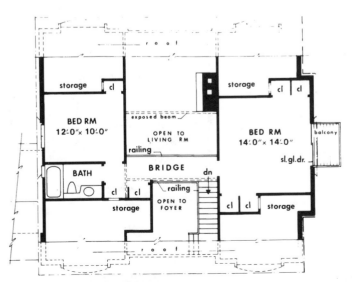

SECOND FLOOR PLAN

First-Floor Master Suite is Special

No. 90624

American as apple pie, this three-bedroom Colonial classic has a welcoming warmth that will capture your fancy. The two-story foyer is lit from above by a skylight. Special features abound throughout the house. Access the terrace or garage through the family room, a convenient kitchen which serves family and formal dining areas with ease, and a heat-circulating fireplace flanked by shelves in the living room. The spacious master suite, housed in a separate wing, has vaulted ceilings and is illuminated by spectacular windows on three walls. With a whirlpool tub and its own entertainment center, this room is bound to be your favorite retreat.

First floor — 1,440 sq. ft.
Second floor — 613 sq. ft.
Basement — 1,340 sq. ft.
Garage — 462 sq. ft.

Total living area — 2,053 sq. ft.

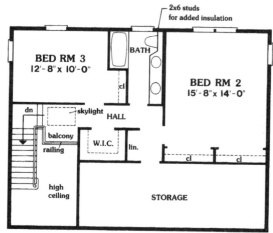

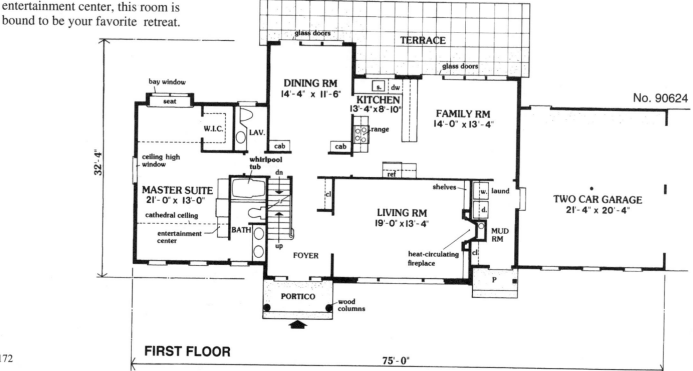

Angled Areas Attract Interest

No. 91708

This home's traditional exterior gives no clue to the creative use of odd angles within. Even though the uniquely-shaped family room is located directly in front of the entryway, the cultured brick wall that backs a woodstove blocks the view into the room. The wall increases energy efficiency by absorbing and holding heat from the woodstove, then radiating it back into the room. The kitchen is visually open to the family room and has an eating nook located at the juncture of the two areas. A triangular-shaped step-in pantry is next to the nook, and the nearby sliding glass doors provide easy access to the deck. Bedrooms and utility room are close to the kitchen. The master suite is at the opposite end of the home, for increased privacy. It has a vaulted-ceiling and a long, dog-leg shaped walk-in closet. The master bath has twin vanities and a huge five-sided custom shower.

Main living area — 1,902 sq. ft.
Garage — 538 sq. ft.

Total living area — 1,902 sq. ft.

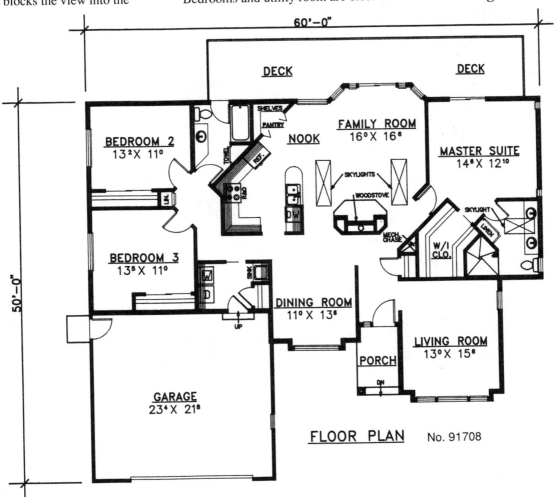

FLOOR PLAN   No. 91708

Varied Roof Heights Create Interesting Lines

No. 90601

This rambling one-story Colonial farmhouse packs a lot of living space into its compact plan. The covered porch, enriched by arches, columns and Colonial details, is the focal point of the facade. Inside, the house is zoned for convenience. Formal living and dining rooms occupy the front of the house. To the rear are the family room, island kitchen, and dinette. The family room features a heat-circulating fireplace, visible from the entrance foyer, and sliding glass doors to the large rear patio. Three bedrooms and two baths are away from the action in a private wing.

Main living area — 1,613 sq. ft.

Total living area — 1,613 sq. ft.

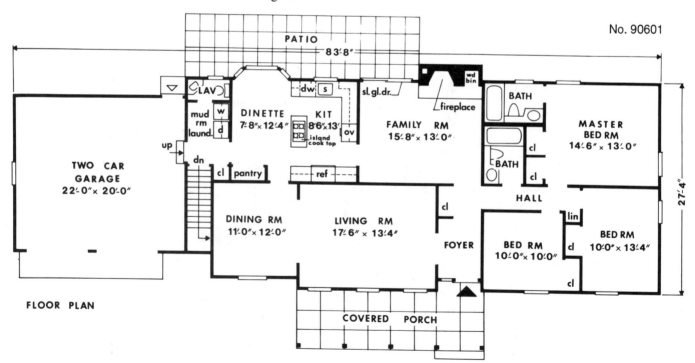

Carefree Comfort
No. 90692

The rustic charm of cedar shingle siding and flowerboxes, the romance of an elegant palladium window, and the warmth of a heat-circulating fireplace add up to a pleasant atmosphere you'll love to come home to. The central foyer sseparates active areas from the bedroom wing, so your privacy is assured. A hallway to the left leads to three bedrooms and two full baths, one in the master suite. To the right lies the sunny living room with its arched window, fireplace, and soaring cathedral ceilings. The kitchen at the rear of the house is flanked by a formal dining room that adjoins the living room, and a cheerful dinette that's ideal for family meals and quick snacks. Sliders in the dining room open to the rear terrace.

Main living area — 1,492 sq. ft.
Garage — 1-car

Total living area — 1,492 sq. ft.

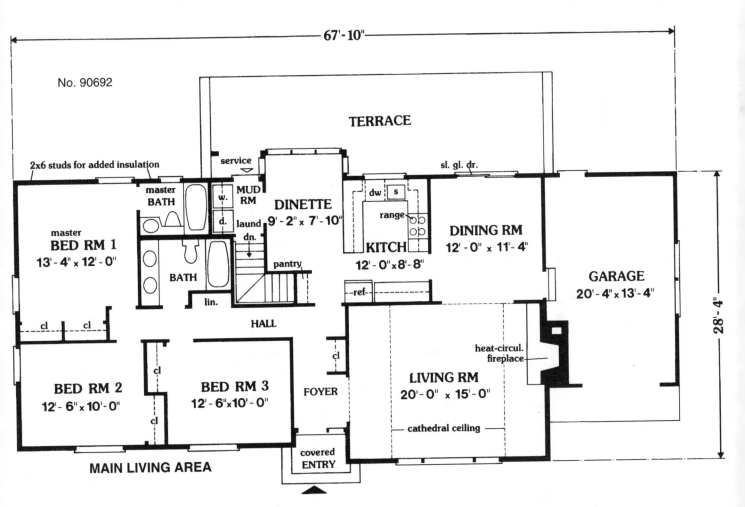

Cozy Traditional With Style

No. 99208

This charming one-story traditional home greets visitors with a covered porch. A galley-style kitchen shares a snack bar with the spacious gathering room where a fireplace is the focal point. An ample master suite includes a luxury bath with a whirlpool tub and separate dressing room. Two additional bedrooms, one that could double as a study, are located at the front of the home.

Basement — 1,830 sq. ft.
Garage — 2-car

Total living area — 1,830 sq. ft.

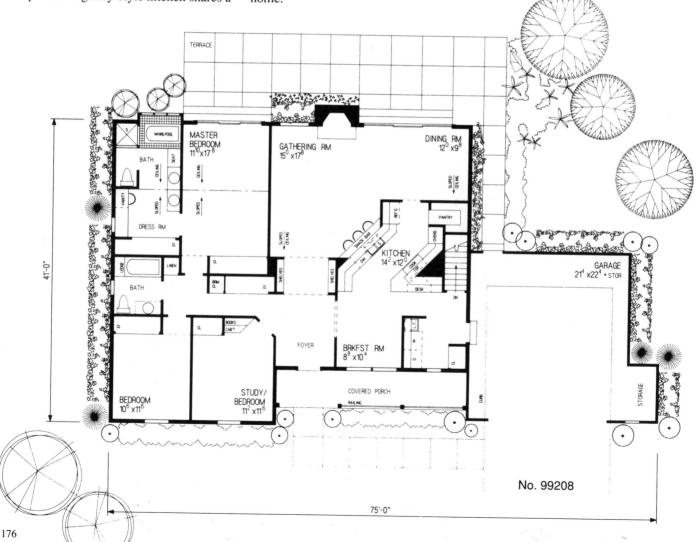

No. 99208

Natural Light Gives Bright Living Spaces

No. 24317

The generous use of windows throughout this home creates bright living spaces. The welcoming covered front porch and lovely bay window give this home great curb appeal. Notice the separate entrance close to the den making a third bedroom a practical possibility. The kitchen has a great center island and large pantry. There is a bright sunny breakfast nook to start your day. The formal dining area is close-by to make entertaining easy. The living room has a fireplace to add atmosphere to the room as well as warmth. There is access to the optional patio from the dining room to add living space. The master bedroom has a private bath and double closets. The second bedroom has ample closet space and shares a full, compartmented hall bath with the possible third bedroom.

Main living area — 1,620 sq. ft.

Total living area — 1,620 sq. ft.

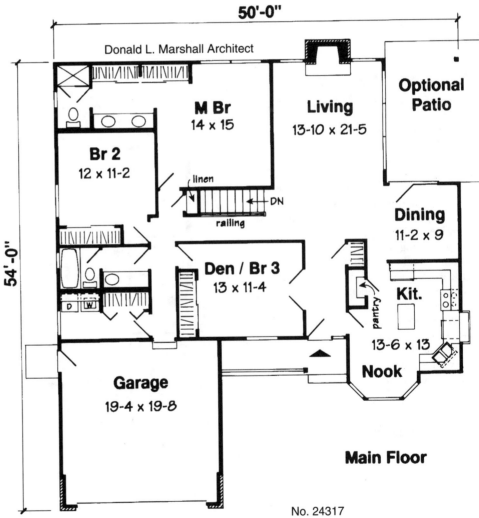

A Celebration of Traditional Elements

No. 10749

Sturdy brick construction, a columned porch, high ceilings with cooling fans, and loads of built-in storage are classic elements from yesterday that make this house special. But, the distinctive interior plan is purely contemporary. Imagine the hushed privacy of the sleeping wing, where every bedroom adjoins a bath, and the skylit master suite enjoys access to the outdoor deck. Look at the central location of the massive, fireplaced family room that also overlooks the deck. And, notice the conveniently-placed island kitchen that serves formal and family areas with equal ease.

Main living area — 3,438 sq. ft.
Garage — 610 sq. ft.

Total living area — 3,438 sq. ft.

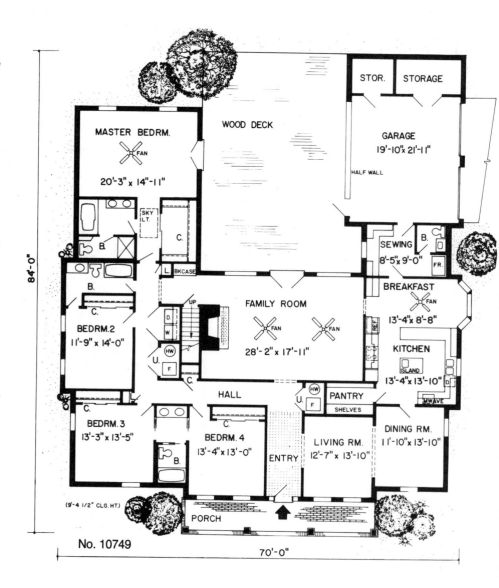

Master Suite Offers Privacy

No. 24318

The large covered porch creates an attractive welcoming entrance. The living room features a volume ceiling treatment accented by a ceiling beam. The dining room adjoins the kitchen and living room making entertaining easy. The large kitchen counter serves as a pass through or a snack bar. There is ample counter and cabinet space with all the amenities you're looking for in a kitchen. There are three bedrooms on this floor sharing the hall full bath. However, upstairs is just for you. The master suite has a floor all of its own. Complete with compartmented master bath, and walk-in closet, this private retreat waits for you at the end of a long day. Imagine having your own private floor away from the noise and problems of the day. The children have their space and you have yours. Seems reasonable.

First floor — 1,008 sq. ft.
Second floor — 367 sq. ft.

Total living area — 1,375 sq. ft.

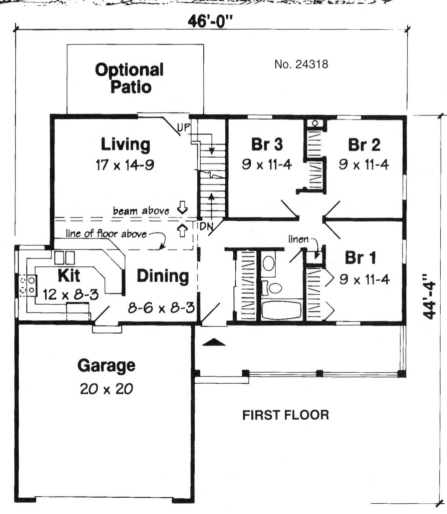

Donald L. Marshall Architect

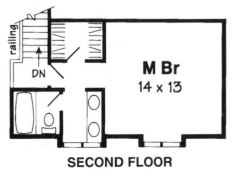

Traditional Interior
No. 24554

In a traditional layout this home provides separate living and dining rooms. There are two coat closets flanking the front door. Having the formal dining room and the breakfast bay area adjoining the kitchen makes service to these rooms simplified. The kitchen features a center island expanding the work area. There is also a double basin sink having a window over it allowing you a view to the backyard. This window is also a great place for plants. The breakfast bay area has easy access to the backyard. The family room features a fireplace and the luxury of built-in bookshelves. Upstairs the master bedroom has a cathedral ceiling, walk-in closet and private master bath. The three secondary bedrooms share the full hall bath. The secondary bedrooms enjoy ample closet space. A traditional layout, yet, conducive to today's untraditional times.

First floor — 1,063 sq. ft.
Second floor — 950 sq. ft.

Total living area — 2,013 sq. ft.

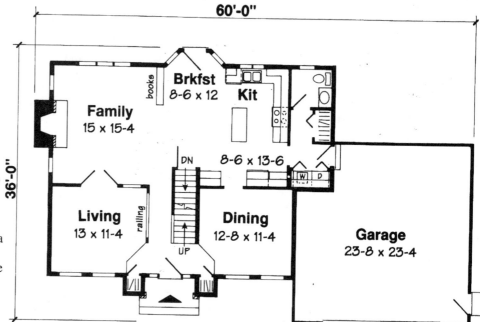

First Floor

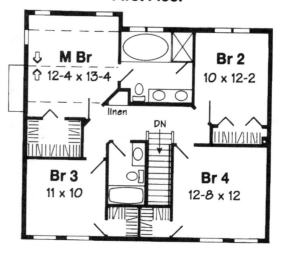

Second Floor

No. 24554

Central Chimney Serves Two Fireplaces

No. 10753

Convenience and elegance combine in this elegant brick Colonial. Entertaining? Formal areas flank the entry for the convenience of your guests. Close the dining room off from the bustle of the busy island-kitchen without compromising efficiency. You'll be proud to show off the massive keeping room with its built-in wetbar and cozy fireplace. Three bedrooms lie up the open staircase, each with its own appealing features. The master suite includes double vanities, a step-in shower, and tub. The rear bedroom enjoys a view of the patio and a walk-in closet. The front bedroom boasts a bookcase wall. And, every room benefits from a chute that delivers dirty clothes right to the laundry room!

First floor — 1,671 sq. ft.
Second floor — 1,134 sq. ft.
Garage — 552 sq. ft.

Total living area — 2,805 sq. ft.

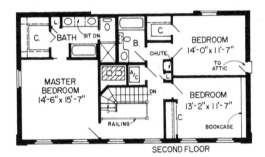

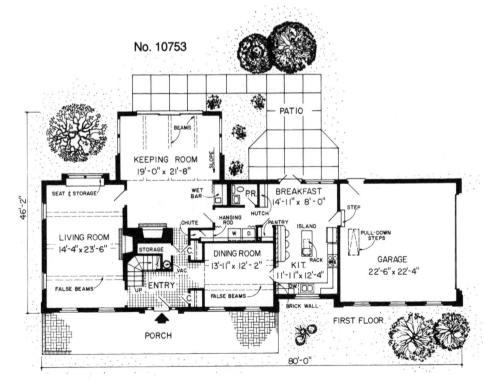

Grace and Convenience

No. 20352

Here's a sprawling Tudor masterpiece that will house your family in comfort and elegance. Features include an airlock vestibule and back-to-back fireplaces serving the formal living room and expansive family room. Built-ins, including the family room planning desk, walk-in pantry, and benched vestibule add immeasurable convenience. When mealtime arrives, enjoy the luxurious ambiance of the bayed dining room, or the cheerful atmosphere of the breakfast room with an entrance to the spacious rear deck. Two well-appointed baths serve the upstairs bedrooms and the vaulted master suite, with its own private deck.

First floor — 1,647 sq. ft.
Second floor — 1,191 sq. ft.
Basement — 1,647 sq. ft.
Garage — 576 sq. ft.

Total living area — 2,838 sq. ft.

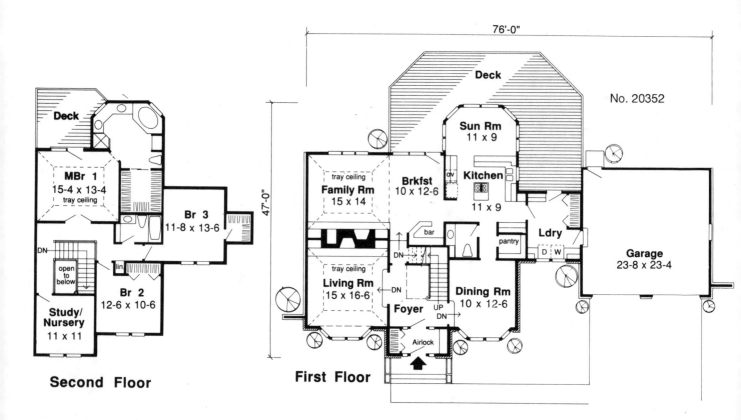

A Country Estate

No. 99605

This English Tudor home portrays the image of a country estate. Besides an attractive exterior and a good functioning plan, it is abound with features such as the decorative circular stair and the curved corners in the foyer; the sunken living room, a regal dining room terminating in a circular bay, a family room with a fireplace, a large pantry closet in the fully equipped kitchen, a lounging porch and a separate dining porch, and a spacious powder room privately located. The second floor features a sitting area which can be used as a library, a master suite consisting of a huge bedroom with large walk-in closets, a study which can be used as a studio, office or retreat room, a bathroom with an oversized whirlpool tub, stall shower and towel closet. The other bedrooms are good size. This house truly lends itself to gracious living.

First Floor — 1,273 sq. ft.
Second Floor — 1,416 sq. ft.
Garage — 2-car

Total living area — 2,689 sq. ft.

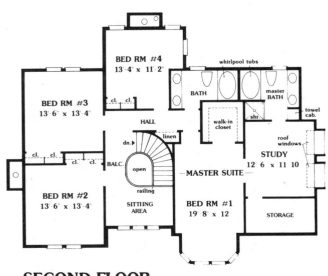

SECOND FLOOR

No. 99605

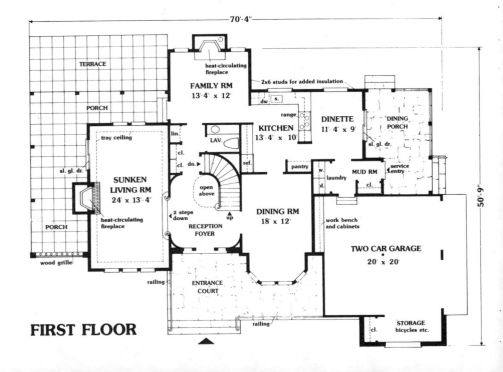

FIRST FLOOR

Beamed Ceiling Accents Family Room

No. 10465

The beamed ceiling, plus the fireplace and built-in bookcase of the comfortable family room, make this design an ideal plan for casual elegance. The family room also shares a wetbar with the adjacent living room. Across the entry from the living room, the dining room is easily accessible from the efficient kitchen. Two bedrooms are aligned along one side with a full bath just steps away, while a guest bedroom contains its own private bath. The master suite is located along the opposite side of the house with its own bath, complete with skylight, and spacious walk-in closet.

Main living area — 2,144 sq. ft.
Garage — 483 sq. ft.

Total living area — 2,144 sq. ft.

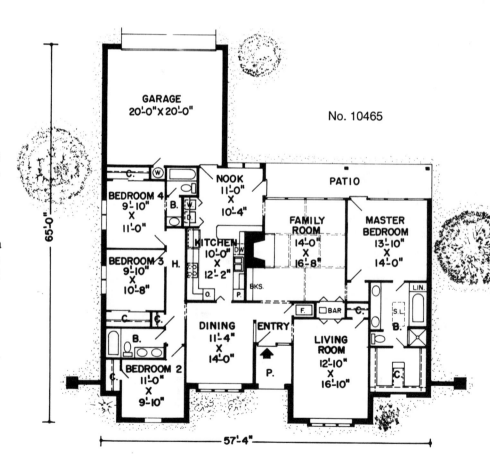

GARAGE PLANS

Save money by Doing-It-Yourself using our Easy-To-Follow plans. Whether you intend to build your own garage or contract it out to a building professional, the Garlinghouse garage plans provide you with everything you need to price out your project and get started. Put our 85 years of experience to work for you.
Order now!!

ITEM NO. 06016C — $86.00
Apartment Garage With One Bedroom

- 24' x 28' Overall Dimensions
- 544 Square Foot Apartment
- 12/12 Gable Roof with Dormers
- Slab or Stem Wall Foundation Options

ITEM NO. 06015C — $86.00
Apartment Garage With Two Bedrooms

- 26' x 28' Overall Dimensions
- 728 Square Foot Apartment
- 4/12 Pitch Gable Roof
- Slab or Stem Wall Foundation Options

ITEM NO. 06012C — $54.00
30' Deep Gable &/or Eave Jumbo Garages

- 4/12 Pitch Gable Roof
- Available Options for Extra Tall Walls, Garage & Personnel Doors, Foundation, Window, & Sidings
- Package contains 4 Different Sizes
- 30' x 28'   • 30' x 32'   • 30' x 36'   • 30' x 40'

ITEM NO. 06013C — $68.00
Two-Car Garage With Mudroom/Breezeway

- Attaches to Any House
- 24' x 24' Eave Entry
- Available Options for Utility Room with Bath, Mudroom, Screened-In Breezeway, Roof, Foundation, Garage & Personnel Doors, Window, & Sidings

ITEM NO. 06001C — $48.00
12', 14', & 16' Wide-Gable 1-Car Garages

- Available Options for Roof, Foundation, Window, Door, & Sidings
- Package contains 8 Different Sizes
- 12' x 20' Mini-Garage • 14' x 22' • 16' x 20' • 16' x 24'
- 14' x 20' • 14' x 24' • 16' x 22' • 16' x 26'

ITEM NO. 06003C — $48.00
24' Wide-Gable 2-Car Garages

- Available Options for Side Shed, Roof, Foundation, Garage & Personnel Doors, Window, & Sidings
- Package contains 5 Different Sizes
- 24' x 22' • 24' x 24' • 24' x 26'
- 24' x 28' • 24' x 32'

ITEM NO. 06007C — $60.00
Gable 2-Car Gambrel Roof Garages

- Interior Rear Stairs to Loft Workshop
- Front Loft Cargo Door With Pulley Lift
- Available Options for Foundation, Garage & Personnel Doors, Window, & Sidings
- Package contains 5 Different Sizes
- 22' x 26' • 22' x 28' • 24' x 28' • 24' x 30' • 24' x 32'

ITEM NO. 06006C — $48.00
22' & 24' Deep Eave 2 & 3-Car Garages

- Can Be Built Stand-Alone or Attached to House
- Available Options for Roof, Foundation, Garage & Personnel Doors, Window, & Sidings
- Package contains 6 Different Sizes
- 22' x 28' • 22' x 32' • 24' x 32'
- 22' x 30' • 24' x 30' • 24' x 36'

ITEM NO. 06002C — $48.00
20' & 22' Wide-Gable 2-Car Garages

- Available Options for Roof, Foundation, Garage & Personnel Doors, Window, & Sidings
- Package contains 7 Different Sizes
- 20' x 20'   • 20' x 24'   • 22' x 22'   • 22' x 28'
- 20' x 22'   • 20' x 28'   • 22' x 24'

ITEM NO. 06008C — $60.00
Eave 2 & 3-Car Clerestory Roof Garages

- Interior Side Stairs to Loft Workshop
- Available Options for Engine Lift, Foundation, Garage & Personnel Doors, Window, & Sidings
- Package contains 4 Different Sizes
- 24' x 26' • 24' x 28' • 24' x 32' • 24' x 36'

Here's What You Get

- Three complete sets of drawings for each plan ordered.
- Detailed step-by-step instructions with easy-to-follow diagrams on how to build your garage (not available with apartment/garages).
- For each garage style, a variety of size and garage door configuration options.
- Variety of roof styles and/or pitch options for most garages.
- Complete materials list.
- Choice between three foundation options: Monolithic Slab, Concrete Stem Wall or Concrete Block Stem Wall.
- Full framing plans, elevations and cross-sectionals for each garage size and configuration.
- And Much More!!

Order Information For Garage Plans:

All garage plan orders contain three complete sets of drawings with instructions and are priced as listed next to the illustration. Additional sets of plans may be obtained for $10.00 each with your original order. UPS shipping is used unless otherwise requested. Please include the proper amount for shipping.

GARLINGHOUSE
Build-It-Yourself PROJECT PLAN

Garage Order Form

Order Code No. G3TR4

My Billing Address is:
Name _____
Address _____
City _____
State _____ Zip _____
Daytime Phone No. _____

Please send me 3 complete sets of the following **GARAGE PLAN**:

Item no. & description	Price
_____	$ _____

Additional Sets
____ (@ $10.00 each) $ _____

Shipping Charges: UPS-$3.75, First Class- $4.50 $ _____

Subtotal: $ _____

Resident sales tax: KS-5.9%, CT-6% $ _____

Total Enclosed: $ _____

My Shipping Address is:
Name _____
Address _____
(UPS will not ship to P.O. Boxes)
City _____
State _____ Zip _____

Send your order to:
(With check or money order payable in U.S. funds only)
The Garlinghouse Company
34 Industrial Park Place
P.O. Box 1717
Middletown, CT 06457

For Faster Service...Charge It!
U.S. & Canada Call
1(800)235-5700
All foreign residents call 1(203)632-0500
❏ Mastercard ❏ Visa ❏ Discover

Card # ☐☐☐☐ ☐☐☐☐ ☐☐☐☐ ☐☐☐☐
Signature _____ Exp. __/__

If paying by credit card, to avoid delays:
billing address must be as it appears on credit card statement
or FAX us at (203) 632-0712

No C.O.D. orders accepted; U.S. funds only. UPS will not ship to Post Office boxes, FPO boxes, APO boxes, Alaska or Hawaii. Canadian orders must be shipped First Class.

Prices subject to change without notice.

Everything You Need to Make

You pay only a fraction of the original cost

You've picked your dream home!

You can already see it standing on your lot... you can see yourselves in your new home... enjoying family, entertaining guests, celebrating holidays. All that remains ahead are the details. That's where we can help. Whether you plan to build-it-yourself, be your own contractor, or hand your plans over to an outside contractor, your Garlinghouse blueprints provide the perfect beginning for putting yourself in your dream home right away.

We even make it simple for you to make professional design modifications. We can also provide a materials list for greater economy.

My grandfather, L.F. Garlinghouse, started a tradition of quality when he founded this company in 1907. For over 85 years, homeowners and builders have relied on us for accurate, complete, professional blueprints. Our plans help you get results fast... and save money, too! These pages will give you all the information you need to order. So get started now... I know you'll love your new Garlinghouse home!

Sincerely,

HERE'S WHAT YOU GET!

Exterior Elevations
Exact scale views of the front, rear and both sides of your home, showing exterior materials, details, and all necessary measurements.

Detailed Floor Plans
Showing the placement of all interior walls, the dimensions of rooms, doors, windows, stairways, and other details.

Typical Wall Sections
Detailed views of your exterior walls, as though sliced from top to bottom. These drawings clarify exterior wall construction insulation, flooring, and roofing details. Depending on your specific geography and climate, your home will be built with either 2x4 or 2x6 exterior walls. Most professional contractors can easily adapt plans for either requirement.

Kitchen and Bath Cabinet Details
These plans or, in some cases, elevations show the specific details and placement of the cabinets in your kitchen and bathrooms as applicable. Customizing these areas is simpler beginning with these details

188

Your Dream Come True!
for home designs by respected professionals.

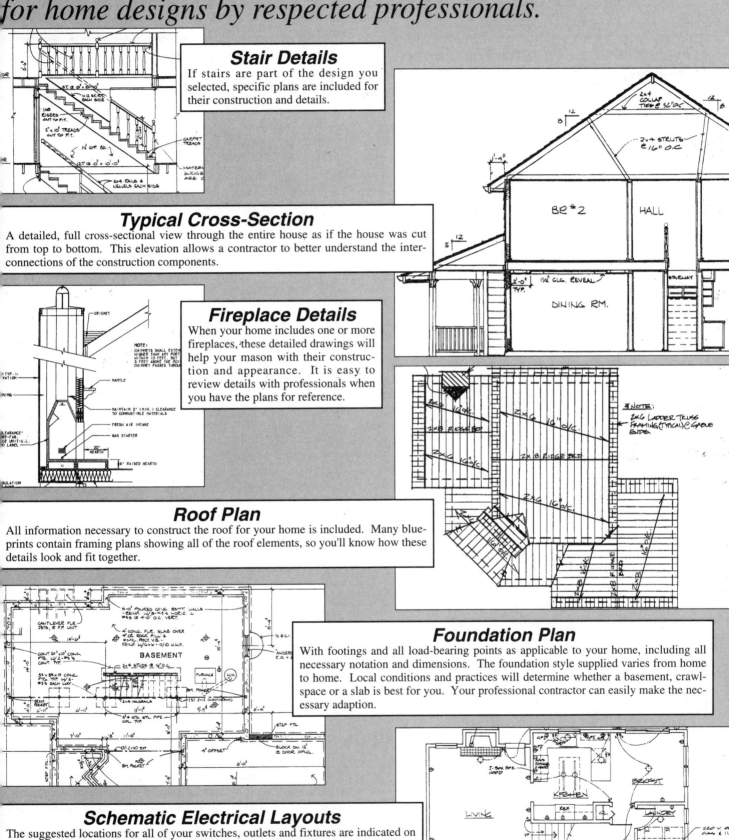

Stair Details
If stairs are part of the design you selected, specific plans are included for their construction and details.

Typical Cross-Section
A detailed, full cross-sectional view through the entire house as if the house was cut from top to bottom. This elevation allows a contractor to better understand the interconnections of the construction components.

Fireplace Details
When your home includes one or more fireplaces, these detailed drawings will help your mason with their construction and appearance. It is easy to review details with professionals when you have the plans for reference.

Roof Plan
All information necessary to construct the roof for your home is included. Many blueprints contain framing plans showing all of the roof elements, so you'll know how these details look and fit together.

Foundation Plan
With footings and all load-bearing points as applicable to your home, including all necessary notation and dimensions. The foundation style supplied varies from home to home. Local conditions and practices will determine whether a basement, crawlspace or a slab is best for you. Your professional contractor can easily make the necessary adaption.

Schematic Electrical Layouts
The suggested locations for all of your switches, outlets and fixtures are indicated on these drawings. They are practical as they are, but they are also a solid taking-off point for any personal adaptions.

Garlinghouse options and extras make the dream truly yours.

Reversed Plans Can Make Your Dream Home Just Right!

"That's our dream home... if only the garage were on the other side!"

You could have exactly the home you want by flipping it end-for-end. Check it out by holding your dream home page of this book up to a mirror. Then simply order your plans "reversed". We'll send you one full set of mirror-image plans (with the writing backwards) as a master guide for you and your builder.

The remaining sets of your order will come as shown in this book so the dimensions and specifications are easily read on the job site... but they will be specially stamped "REVERSED" so there is no construction confusion.

We can only send reversed plans with multiple-set orders. But, there is no extra charge for this service.

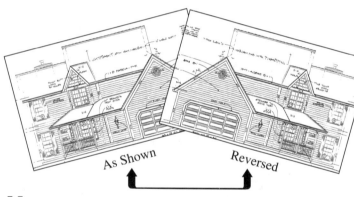

As Shown / Reversed

Modifying Your Garlinghouse Home Plan

Easy modifications to your dream home... minor non-structural changes, simple material substitutions... can be made between you and your builder.

However, if you are considering making major changes to your design, we strongly recommend that you use an architect or a professional designer. And, since you have already started with our complete detailed blueprints, the cost of those expensive professional services will be significantly less.

Our Reproducible Vellums Make Modifications Easier

They provide a design professional with the right way to make changes directly to your Garlinghouse home plans and then print as many copies of the modified plans as you need. The price is $395 plus shipping. Call 1-800-235-5700 to find out more.

Yours FREE With Your Order

FREE SPECIFICATIONS AND CONTRACT FORM provides the perfect way for you and your builder to agree on the exact materials to use in building and finishing your home *before* you start construction. A must for homeowner's peace of mind.

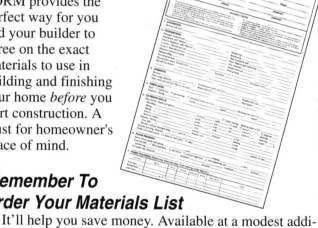

Remember To Order Your Materials List

It'll help you save money. Available at a modest additional charge, the Materials List gives the quantity, dimensions, and specifications for the major materials needed to build your home. You will get faster, more accurate bids from your contractors and building suppliers — and avoid paying for unused materials and waste. Materials Lists are available for all home plans except as otherwise indicated, but can only be ordered with a set of home plans. Due to differences in regional requirements and homeowner or builder preferences... electrical, plumbing and heating/air conditioning equipment specifications are not designed specifically for each plan. However, detailed *typical* prints of residential electrical, plumbing and construction guidelines can be provided. Each set of electrical and plumbing prints conforms to the requirements at the National Electrical and Plumbing Codes. The construction prints conform to the Uniform Building Code or BOCA code. These prints can be supplied at a low cost of $14.95 each.

Questions?

Call our customer service number at 1-203-632-0500.

How Many Sets Of Plans Will You Need?

The Standard 8-Set Construction Package
Our experience shows that you'll speed every step of construction and avoid costly building errors by ordering enough sets to go around. Each tradesperson wants a set — the general contractor and all subcontractors; foundation, electrical, plumbing, heating/air conditioning, drywall, finish carpenters, and cabinet shop. Don't forget your lending institution, building department and, of course, a set for yourself.

The Minimum 5-Set Construction Package
If you're comfortable with arduous follow-up, this package can save you a few dollars by giving you the option of passing down plan sets as work progresses. You might have enough copies to go around if work goes exactly as scheduled and no plans are lost or damaged. But for only $30 more, the 8-set package eliminates these worries.

The Single-Set Decision-Maker Package
We offer this set so you can study the blueprints to plan your dream home in detail. But remember... one set is never enough to build your home... and they're copyrighted.

New Plan Details For The Home Builder
Because local codes and requirements vary greatly, we recommend that you obtain drawings and bids from licensed contractors to do your mechanical plans. However, if you want to know more about techniques — and deal more confidently with subcontractors — we offer these remarkably useful detail sheets. Each is an excellent tool that will enhance your understanding of these technical subjects.

Residential Construction Details
Eight sheets that cover the essentials of stick-built residential home construction. Details foundation options - poured concrete basement, concrete block, or monolithic concrete slab. Shows all aspects of floor, wall, and roof framing. Provides details for roof dormers, eaves, and skylights.

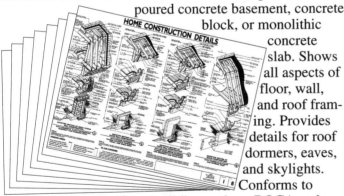

Conforms to requirements of Uniform Building code or BOCA code. Includes a quick index. *$14.95 per set*

Residential Plumbing Details
Nine sheets packed with information detailing pipe connection methods, fittings, and sizes. Shows sump-pump and water softener hookups, and septic system construction. Conforms to requirements

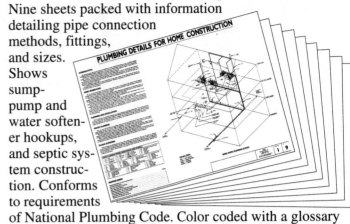

of National Plumbing Code. Color coded with a glossary of terms and quick index. *$14.95 per set*

Residential Electrical Details
Nine sheets that cover all aspects of residential wiring, from simple switch wiring to the complexities of three-phase and service entrance connection. Explains service load calculations and distribution panel wiring. Shows you how to create a floor-plan wiring diagram. Conforms to requirements of National Electrical Code. Color coded with a glossary of terms and a quick index. *$14.95 per set*

Important Shipping Information
Your order is processed immediately. Allow 10 working days from our receipt of your order for normal UPS delivery. Save time with your credit card and our "800" number. UPS *must* have a street address or Rural Route Box number — never a post office box. Use a work address if no one is home during the day.

Orders being shipped to Alaska, Hawaii, APO, FPO or Post Office Boxes must go via First Class Mail. Please include the proper postage.

Overseas checks, money orders, or international money transfers must be payable in U.S. currency. For speed, we ship international orders Air Parcel Post. Please refer to the chart for the correct shipping cost.

An important note:
All plans are drawn to conform to one or more of the industry's major national building standards. However, due to the variety of local building regulations, your plan may need to be modified to comply with local requirements — snow loads, energy loads, seismic zones, etc. Do check them fully and consult your local building officials.

A few states require that all building plans used be drawn by an architect registered in that state. While having your plans reviewed and stamped by such an architect may be prudent, laws requiring non-conforming plans like ours to be completely redrawn forces you to unnecessarily pay very large fees. If your state has such a law, we strongly recommend you contact your state representative to protest.

Blueprint Price Schedule

Standard Construction Package (8 sets)	$255.00
Minimum Construction Package (5 sets)	$225.00
Single-Set Package	$180.00
Each Additional Set (ordered w/one above)	$ 20.00
Materials List (with plan order only)	$ 25.00

Domestic Shipping	
UPS Ground Service	$ 7.00
First Class Mail	$ 8.50
Express Delivery Service — Call For Details 1-800-235-5700	

International Shipping	One Set	Mult. Sets
Canada	$ 7.25	$12.50
All Other Nations	$18.50	$50.00

Canadian orders are now Duty Free.

Canadian Orders and Shipping:

To our friends in Canada, we have a plan design affiliate in Kitchener, Ontario. This relationship will help you avoid the delays and charges associated with shipments from the United States. Moreover, our affiliate is familiar with the building requirements in your community and country.

We prefer payments in U.S. Currency. If you, however, are sending Canadian funds please add 30% to the prices of the plans and shipping fees.

Please Submit all Canadian plan orders to:
Garlinghouse Company
20 Cedar Street North
Kitchener, Ontario N2H 2W8

Canadian orders only: 1-800-561-4169
Fax #: 1-519-743-1282
Customer Service #: 1-519-743-4169

Before ordering **PLEASE READ** all ordering information

ORDER TOLL FREE
1-800-235-5700

Monday-Friday 8:00 a.m. to 5:00 p.m. Eastern Time
or FAX your Credit Card order to 1-203-632-0712
All foreign residents call 1-203-632-0500.

Please have ready:
1. Your credit card number
2. The plan number
3. The order code number

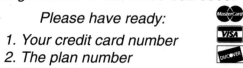

Blueprint Order Form

Order Code No. **H3TR4**

Prices Subject To Change Without Notice

Send your check, money order or credit card information to:

Please Submit all United States & Other Nations plan orders to:
Garlinghouse Company
34 Industrial Park Place, P.O. Box 1717
Middletown, CT 06457

Please Submit all Canadian plan orders to:
Garlinghouse Company
20 Cedar Street North
Kitchener, Ontario N2H 2W8

Plan No. _____

❑ As Shown ❑ Reversed (mult. set pkgs. only)

	Each	Amount
8 set pkg.	$255.00	$
5 set pkg.	$225.00	$
1 set pkg. (no reverses)	$180.00	$
___ (qty.) Add'l. sets @	$ 20.00	$
Material List	$ 25.00	$
Residential Builder Plans		
___ set(s) Construction @	$ 14.95	$
___ set(s) Plumbing @	$ 14.95	$
___ set(s) Electrical @	$ 14.95	$
Shipping — see chart		$
Subtotal		$
Sales Tax (CT residents add 6% sales tax, KS residents add 5.9% sales tax)		$
Total Amount Enclosed		$

Bill To: (address must be as it appears on credit card statement)

Name _____
    Please Print

Address _____

City/State _____ Zip _____

Daytime Phone (___) _____

Ship To (if different from Bill to):

Name _____

Address _____
    UPS will not ship to P.O. Boxes

City/State _____ Zip _____

Credit Card Information

Charge To: ❑ Visa   ❑ Mastercard   ❑ Discover

Card # |__|__|__|__|__|__|__|__|__|__|__|__|__|__|__|__|

Signature _____ Exp. ___/___

Thank your for your order!

Garlinghouse plans are copyright protected. Purchaser hereby agrees that the home plan construction drawings being purchased will not be used for the construction of more than one single dwelling, and that these drawings will not be reproduced either in whole or in part by any means whatsoever.